FABERGÉ

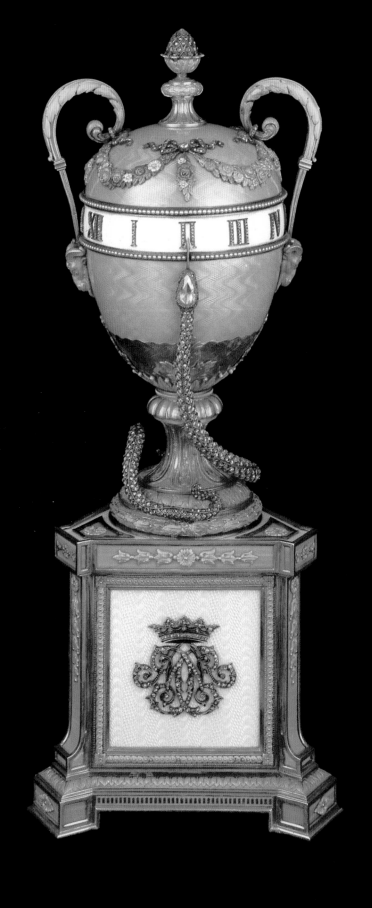

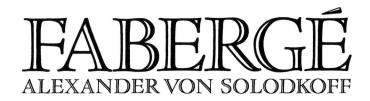

FABERGÉ
ALEXANDER VON SOLODKOFF

BB Bounty
BOOKS

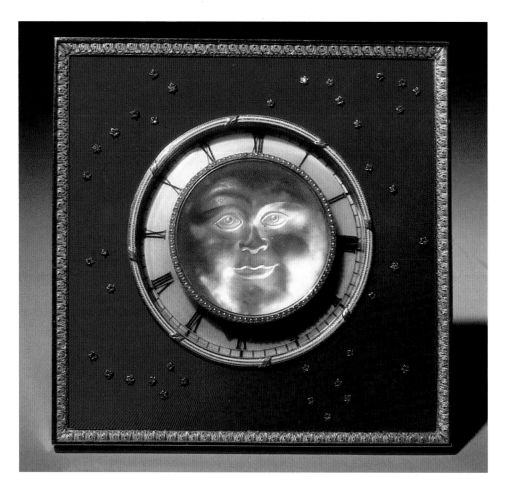

First published in 1988 by Pyramid

This edition published 2005 by Bounty Books,
a division of Octopus Publishing Group Ltd
2–4 Heron Quays, London E14 4JP

Copyright © Alexander von Solodkoff

ISBN 0 7537 1167 2
ISBN13 9780753711675

A CIP catalogue record for this book is available
from the British Library

Printed and bound in China

CONTENTS

INTRODUCTION

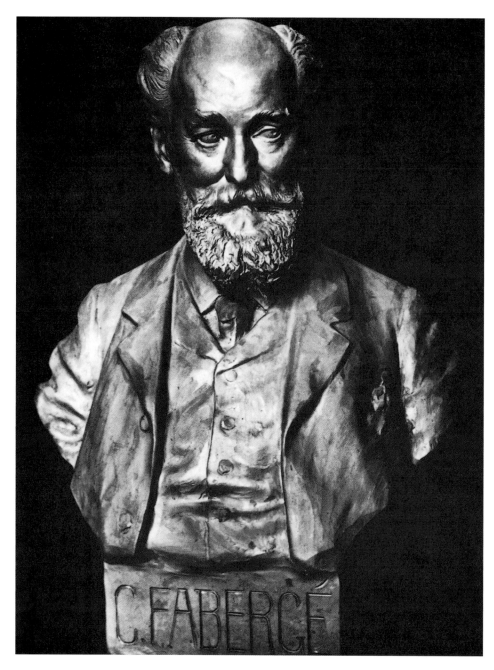

Portrait bust of Carl Fabergé by Joseph Limburg, 1903

Fabergé's work has always aroused delight and fascination. But Fabergé has also often been regarded as the jeweller of a decadent, autocratic regime, the creator of luxuries that are vain symbols of princely magnificence.

Today he is seen in a different light, a light cast by further studies in the fields of history and of artistic influence. His place in art history is that of an exceptionally creative artist-jeweller with outstanding entrepreneurial skill.

The growth of Fabergé's firm — from a small jewellery business to a company employing up to 500 artists and workers — was not due solely to the patronage of the Tsars and a handful of aristocrats. Its success was based on the economic boom that Russia enjoyed in the second half of the 19th century. Easter eggs of Imperial size were commissioned not only by the Tsar, but also by industrialists and many less important pieces were bought by the increasingly wealthy bourgeoisie. As Christopher Forbes has argued, Fabergé's creations should not be seen as frivolous playthings of a decadent regime, but rather as manifestations of Russia's economic vitality during the late 19th and early 20th centuries.

Another sign of change in the interpretation of Fabergé's work is perhaps the increasing number of articles published by Soviet authors — writers who for political reasons had previously considered Fabergé scarcely worthy of attention. Lenin's cultural commissar Lunacharsky is said to have expressed the opinion that no object which had been touched by a member of the last Tsar's family could have ever have historical value. The days of such revolutionary views seem to be over. Soviet writers now justly emphasize the importance of the Russian artistic traditions that so influenced Fabergé. All agree that he produced works of art of exceptional inventiveness and technical perfection.

Many books and articles have described Fabergé's art in great detail. Since the late 1970s there have been several new discoveries of original material in archives and from other sources. These include details about the commissioning of the first Imperial Easter egg and the discovery of the the sales ledgers of Fabergé's London branch.

The art historian's view of Fabergé, upon which attention was focused by the 1986 exhibition in Munich, has led to an increased interest in his stylistic sources from within Russia, as well as from western Europe and Japan. *Fabergé style* and *Fabergé design* are terms which are now generally accepted, although they are often used as attempts to express the indefinable and exotic side of Fabergé's *oeuvre*.

These subjects have recently been discussed in a number of monographs, articles and catalogues, all of great interest to the specialist.

This book is an attempt to summarize some of the research made during the last ten years by Fabergé specialists. It provides basic information on Fabergé's life and work together with all the important recent discoveries, some of which point towards a new interpretation of his *oeuvre*.

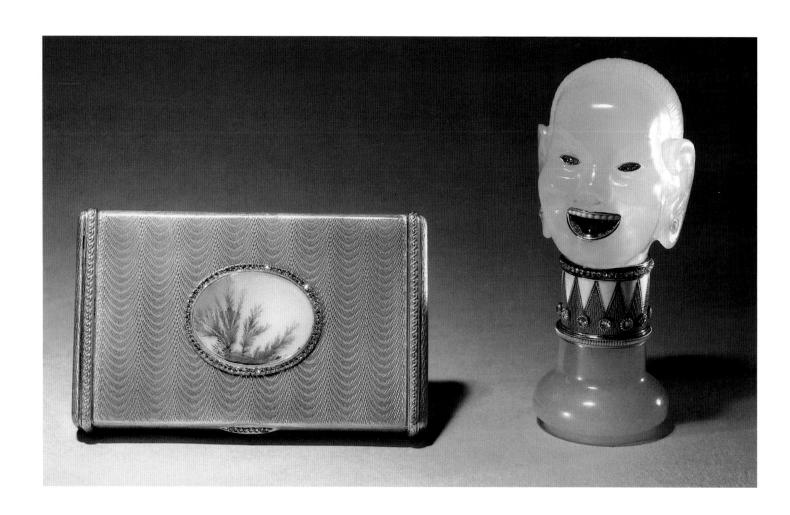

Left: *Enamelled cigarette case, the
cover inset with a moss agate plaque.
Workmaster, Henrik Wigström. It was
sold at Fabergé's London branch on
13 January 1914 for £14.*
Right: *Jewelled, gold-mounted, jade desk
seal with head of a laughing Chinaman.
8.9 cm (3½ inches)*

Chapter One

FABERGÉ STYLE AND DESIGN

Fabergé's youthful studies of the great collections of Europe had given him an intimate knowledge of the artistic and technical diversity of the past. Stylistic influences ranging from classical antiquity to art nouveau can be seen in his work, and many national styles are reflected. Experts hold that his finest work developed the classical French styles characteristic of the Louis XVI and Empire periods. A true Fabergé item has a quality of style and workmanship: it seems to look you in the eye and assert with insouciant confidence 'I am a Fabergé'.

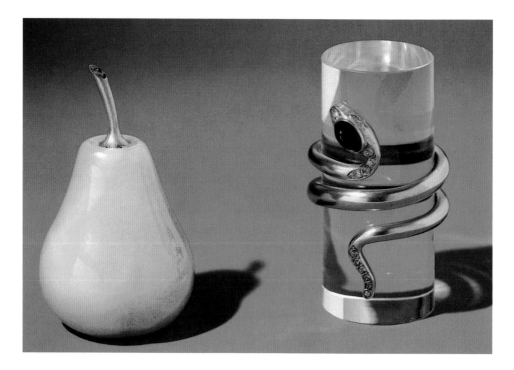

Fabergé specialists and connoisseurs have always maintained that they can easily recognize a genuine Fabergé object, even without studying the marks or the signature; and similarly, that they can equally readily identify a forgery. When asked they always say straightaway that it is the exceptional quality of the workmanship which distinguishes a real Fabergé piece.

But the quality of some of the forgeries can be deceptive. The experts' judgement is also based on the fact that there is a certain style or design which makes an original Fabergé piece so unmistakable. Géza von Habsburg described it in his chapter 'Fabergé Design' in the remarkable 1987 Munich Fabergé exhibition catalogue:

Another secret of his work is the fact that all his objects clearly bear the

Left: Bowenite gluepot in the shape of a pear. The gold stem is the brush handle.
Right: *Jewelled desk seal*

imprint of his personality, whatever the style they were made in. Whether produced by Kollin, Perchin or Wigström, whether classical, Renaissance, baroque or Empire in form, Fabergé blended these opposites together in such a way that an easily identifiable style emerged. The Fabergé style is absolutely his own and one that has never been satisfactorily imitated.

How can this distinctive style or design be defined? First we have to examine the personality of the master Carl Fabergé himself, his educational background and artistic training.

The foundations for his artistic development had been laid during his years of study in Paris, Dresden and Florence. As a young man Fabergé had studied, for example, the collections of the Green Vaults in Dresden which included *Kunstkammer* objects, curiosities and works of art of the 16th and 17th centuries, including enamelled Renaissance jewellery and hardstone carving from Saxony. The magnificent and sometimes rather grotesque looking enamelled and gold-mounted pieces by Johann Melchior Dinglinger, whose miniature version of the Court of the Moghul Sultan is in the Green Vaults, left a strong impression on Fabergé. So too did the late 18th century work of Johann Christian Neuber, especially his hardstone mosaic snuff boxes. These were sources not only of Fabergé's

artistic inspiration, but also of the perfectionism that he brought to his own work. He was also influenced by the collections in the Pitti Palace in Florence – figures and reliefs in polychrome marble, hardstones from the Opificio delle Pietre Dure, and the Medici collection of Renaissance hardstone vessels and enamelled jewels. The Gothic element in some of Fabergé's pieces may well have come from the years of his apprenticeship in Frankfurt.

Probably the strongest influence on Fabergé's work was the treasury of the Hermitage in St Petersburg, where the collections of the tsars were kept. These included a hoard of Scythian gold

Silver tea and coffee service in a baroque revivalist style, circa 1890

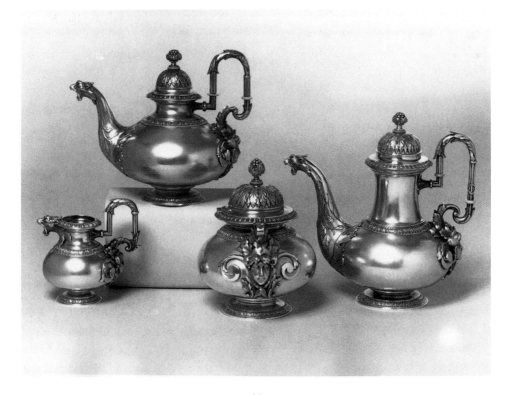

and major works by the goldsmiths of Paris and Berlin – jewelled snuffboxes, enamelled watches and the collection of gold-mounted and jewelled walking-sticks which had belonged to Catherine the Great. Many of these had been made in the French style by Russian goldsmiths and jewellers in the 18th century. Fabergé was familar with the Hermitage treasury from his early years and later on, after he had been given the title 'Jeweller to His Majesty and the Imperial Hermitage' in 1885 had constant access to it.

Fabergé's artistic education had been wide-ranging and, like the arts in general of his time, eclectic. He had studied not only the styles of the past, but also the techniques of the goldsmith's art in most of the great centres and important collections of Europe. Those studies had focussed his attention on the elements of fantasy and the unusual in the stylistic diversity of the past.

Mir Iskusstva

The arts and their interrelationships became the guiding idea of a movement in Russia known as *Mir Iskusstva*, (World of Art). It was founded in 1889 as an association of artists and writers with members such as Serge Diaghilev, Alexandre Benois and Konstantin Somov. *Mir Iskusstva*, in opposition to the heavily nationalistic art informed by Pan-Slavic ideals and the spirit of Old Russia, sought to revive the artistic and cultural traditions of 18th and early 19th century Europe. It turned St Petersburg into a Russian artistic centre

of international stature. Interests of this movement included theatrical design (mainly for the *Ballet Russe*), impressionism in painting and modernism in sculpture, and extended to the applied arts such as porcelain design and manufacture. Fabergé's links with the World of Art movement are thought to have arisen from his friendship with Alexander Benois, who supplied him with ideas and designs including that of the 1905 Colonnade Easter Egg.

One surprising fact about Fabergé's work is that no design or even finished work from his own hand is known to exist. Our knowledge of what consitutes the Fabergé style can be based only on the production of the Fabergé workshops.

In the earlier period, from about 1870 to 1885, Fabergé seems to have been very much dependent on a revival of interest in the antique. He made heavy gold objects and jewellery in the antique style and his artefacts can be compared with the work of Castellani, who specialised in objects in the Etruscan style which had become fashionable after 1867 when they had been exhibited at the Paris World Fair by Eugène Fontenay.

Fabergé had seen the gold treasure consisting of Greek antique objects of the 4th century BC which had been discovered at Kerch in the Crimea in 1867. On the suggestion of Count Sergei Stroganoff, the president of the Imperial Archaeological Commission, he had copied a number of these antique gold objects and exhibited them with great success at the 1885 Nuremberg exhibition. A typical example of this style is the twisted gold bangle with two lion finials, which is now in the Forbes Collection in New York.

From 1885 onwards there followed a production of *objets d'art* in ancient styles of varied origin reflecting the eclecticism typical of the time. The Celtic style is represented by heavy torque bracelets made of the purest gold or silver set at the ends with two large single stones such as rubies and sapphires.

An example of Fabergé's work imitating the Merovingian style of the 7th century was revealed recently at the Munich National Museum (and discussed by Géza von Habsburg in an article in *Kunst & Antiquitäten*.) It was a pectoral cross set with cabochon sapphires and pearls and inspired by the jewelled cross of the Merovingian King Reccesvinthus (649–72) which Fabergé must have seen in Paris at the Musée de Cluny, where it was kept.

One example of the Gothic style is a miniature casket of gold-mounted nephrite, probably inspired by an enamelled Limoges reliquary of the 13th century.

The Renaissance period also fascinated jewellers of the late 19th century. They were intrigued by its excellence in extremely difficult enamel techniques such as the *email en ronde bosse* where a curved surface or relief is covered by enamel. Goldsmiths in Germany such as Reinhold Vasters, now recognized as a brilliant copier of Renaissance jewellery, Hermann Ratzersdorfer in Vienna and Heinrich

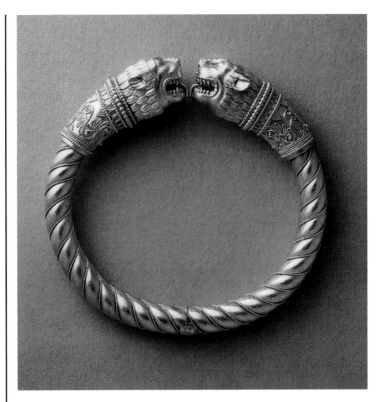

Gold bangle in the archaeological style, a copy after a bracelet from the Kerch treasure by Erik Kollin, circa 1885

Kautsch in Budweis, are examples of artists working in the Renaissance style which prevailed in the jeweller's art between 1870 and 1890.

Fabergé created a number of exquisite objects in this style which are lavishly enamelled and encrusted with precious stones in typical collet mounts. They were, however, never intended as direct copies and in many cases appear more elegantly modelled. One example is the Resurrection Easter Egg – the design of a 16th century reliquary transformed into an egg.

The coronation present to the Tsar from the nobility of St Petersburg in

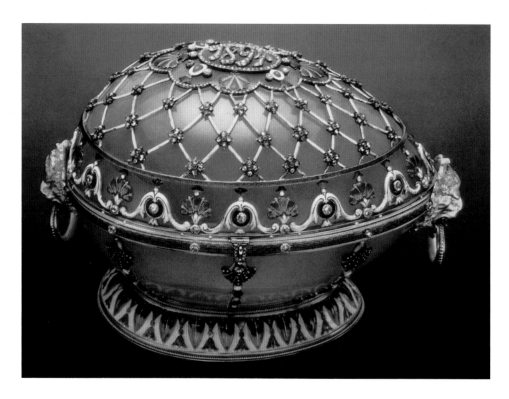

The Imperial Renaissance Easter Egg by Michael Perchin, dated 1894. 14 cm (5¼ inches). (Forbes Collection)

1896 was a large oval dish of engraved rock crystal with jewelled and enamelled matt gold mounts in the Renaissance style, of which the prototype is said to be in the Kunsthistorisches Museum in Vienna. An oblong nephrite tray with jewelled and enamelled handles in similar Renaissance style was the wedding present of the Dutch colony of St Petersburg to Queen Wilhelmina of the Netherlands in 1901. The Coronation Vase, an engraved rock crystal vase given by Leopold de Rothschild to Queen Mary in 1911, also follows the Renaissance idiom with colourfully enamelled jewelled gold mounts.

All these 'retrospective' styles, including the French Regency style, epitomised by the 1894 Imperial Easter Egg and based on the Le Roy *bonbonière* from the Green Vaults in Dresden are

The Imperial Renaissance Easter Egg by Michael Perchin, dated 1894. 14 cm (5¼ inches). (Forbes Collection)

exceptional items in Fabergé's *oeuvre*; they are not representative of his work as a whole.

Before we discuss the more typical French styles of the 18th and early 19th centuries, which influenced Fabergé enormously and in which the majority of his objects are made, we must mention the influence of the exotic styles – the Chinese, Egyptian, Moorish and Persian. Fabergé would pick up ideas from historical styles, and he even made use of objects from other periods and cultures: Chinese snuff bottles or Moghul dagger handles were remounted as perfume bottles or paperknives. The use of such styles reflects his

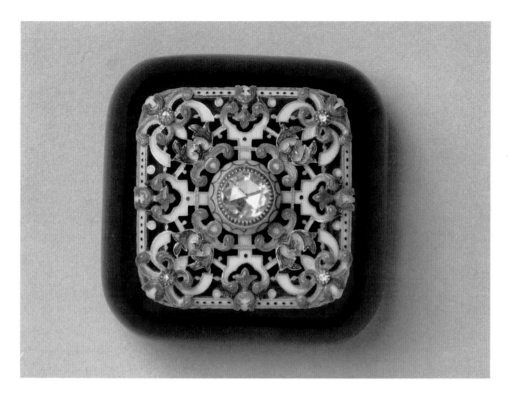

Cover of a bonbonnière in the Renaissance style, decorated with enamel and set with a large rose-cut diamond

studies of the historical collections of the courts of France, Saxony and Medici Florence. In a sense he was following the example of the 16th century prince, creating in his work a *Wunderkammer*, a collection of sometimes bizarre and exotic items which are valuable not so much for their intrinsic worth but for their rarity or curiosity.

The majority of Fabergé's objects are in the French Empire style or in the baroque or classical styles of Louis XV or Louis XVI. Whereas most objects with rococo scrolls can be attributed to the period between 1890 and 1905, many objects dating from around 1900 have a curious combination of the Louis XV and the art nouveau style with foliage and plant motifs interwoven with rococo scrolls. Objects with the more classical decoration of laurel and palmette bands, bows and flower garlands may be dated between 1905 and 1915, when the Fabergé production reached its peak. It is not surprising that these styles revived the art of enamelling in the *guilloché* technique originally practised by the French 18th century goldsmiths and at which Fabergé so greatly excelled. It was particularly for his achievements with this technique, which even the French no longer practised to such perfection, that he was made a *maître* of the Parisian goldsmith's guild at the *Exposition Universelle* in 1900.

The neo-classical taste was very much an international trend at the time

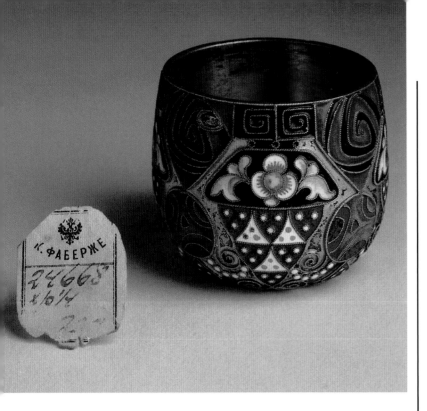

Vodka cup in the old Russian style with its original label showing the inventory number. (Forbes Collection)

and can readily be found in many English *objets d'art* of around 1910. It is probably one reason for Fabergé's popularity with Edwardian society.

With the Empire style Fabergé was following a Russian fashion which had its origins in the centenary of Napoleon's retreat from Moscow, which was celebrated with great pomp in 1912. This style revived the sphinxes, laurel wreaths and other classical motifs of the Russian and French Empire period in fashion around 1810.

Bainbridge, in his article in *The Connoisseur* in 1934 on Russian Imperial Easter gifts, came to the conclusion that Fabergé's 'greatest inspiration, however, came from Russia itself, and just as she assimilated foreign styles and evolved something from them to accord with her own tastes, so Russia impressed her stamp on Fabergé.'

Russia's strongest stylistic influence on Fabergé came at the time of the Romanov Tercentenary in 1913, although the Muscovite or Old Russian style, which had obtained official recognition at the 1882 Pan-Russian Exhibition sponsored by Alexander III, had always been represented in his *oeuvre*. This style, reviving the decorative motifs of the 17th century before the time of Peter the Great, is clearly represented in such typically Russian items as icons, *kovsh* and bowls in the *bratina* shape. These were often decorated in the polychrome *cloisonné* enamel technique, with filigree ornaments or chased stylized trailing flowers of a more oriental aspect.

Art Nouveau

The theme of flowers and plants brings us back to the international stylistic development of the time, which was very much under the spell of the art nouveau movement. Fabergé followed to a great extent essential stylistic elements based on Japanese art, which as a fashion had preceded art nouveau by about 20 years. The elegance of Japanese design and artistic expression can be seen in many aspects of Fabergé's *oeuvre*. It is not merely the flower studies or netsuke-like hardstone animals that reveal Japanese influence. To see small *objets d'art* as a source of aesthetic pleasure is itself part of Japanese culture. Technically, too, the Japanese art of combining varicoloured metals was highly admired by European goldsmiths at the time and this also had its effect on Fabergé's work.

When the Japanese influence was transformed in Paris into the *'style moderne'* or art nouveau around 1900, it was a new style for which Fabergé showed no great enthusiasm. This can probably be attributed to the strong conservatism of Russian society, which did not readily take to this modern movement in the arts. However, those objects which Fabergé did create in the art nouveau idiom reflect his acute eye for the artistic value of the style. Some of them, especially the jewellery and the Imperial Pansy and Clover Easter Eggs of 1899 and 1902, rank among the finest work produced in this style in Europe.

The majority of Fabergé's art nouveau objects were functional silver pieces, such as cutlery or mounted carafes, nearly all of them produced in the Moscow workshops. More decorative items such as desk sets with scenes from fairy tales or historical events interpreted in a Russian version of the art nouveau style, are probably due to the influence of artists such as the painters Wrubel and Roerich.

It was probably to keep up with the increasingly important art nouveau movement that in about 1910 Fabergé sent one of his workmasters, Derbyshev, at his own expense to Paris to study under René Lalique, the artistic leader of this style.

Finally there are certain pieces that are so completely original in shape and design that they can be called neither

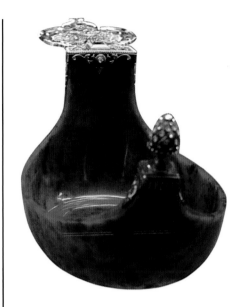

Jewelled, nephrite kovsh *presented by Tsar Nicholas II to Sultan Abdul Hamid II. Workmaster, Michael Perchin. (Topkapi Museum, Istanbul)*

'historical' nor art nouveau. These objects, without ornamentation, embody the notion of practical utility in its purest form. Examples are the cigarette cases and étuis in completely smooth or ribbed gold, set only with a cabochon stone which is intended less for decorative purposes than to serve as a push-button for opening the case. In addition to these cigarette cases, for which Fabergé became famous and which are still widely imitated today, he also produced powder compacts, boxes, and silver items such as tea and coffee services which are characterized by plain and purely functional shapes. This forward-looking style, striking in its simplicity, heralds the art deco style of the 1920s. Similarly there are some jewellery pieces – brooches and pendants – that look as though they were made by Cartier in Paris during the 1920s, although they are in Holmström's stockbook as early as 1913.

The technical side of the firm's production also deserves closer examination. How and by whom the objects were designed in the first instance is a puzzling problem. Was Fabergé himself the outstanding creator-artist?

Although we do not know of designs by Fabergé or objects that he had made with his own hands, there can be no doubt that he was strongly involved in the creation of his objects. The way production took shape can best be understood from the recollections of Henry C. Bainbridge, who knew Fabergé, the workmasters and their workshops. What follows is based on his reminiscences published in *The Connoisseur* in 1934–5.

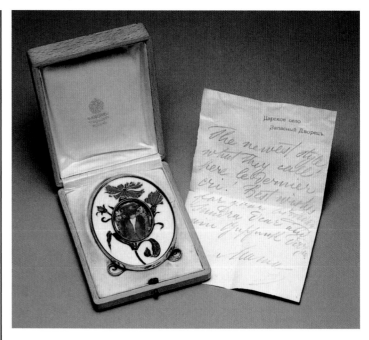

When a particularly important item was about to be made, one of the large Easter eggs, for example, Fabergé first made a rough sketch. Whilst his brother Agathon was known as the most talented designer of the firm from 1882 until his death in 1895, his son Eugène from 1895 worked in collaboration with his father on initial ideas. These were then transformed by the designers into a working drawing. One of the best designers was apparently his second son, another Agathon, who was a superb judge of precious stones. The

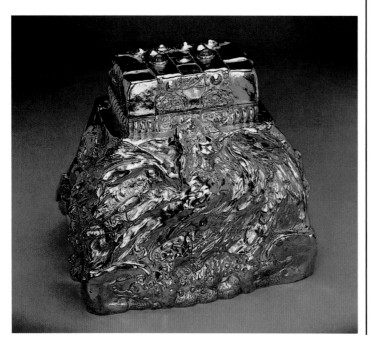

Left: Silver desk inkwell in the Russian art nouveau style 20 cm (8 inches)
Above: Art nouveau photograph frame enamelled with cornflowers 8.3 cm (3¼ inches) A present from the Grand Duchess Marie to her daughter Princess Alexandra zu Hohenlohe-Langenburg with a note from the Grand Duchess on paper headed Tsarkoe Selo

firm's chief designer was François Birbaum, a Swiss, whose versatility and talents Bainbridge praised very highly. Birbaum was assisted in the studios by Alexander Ivashov, Oskar May and Eugen Jacobson.

The design was then put into the hands of the workmasters. Most of them had their workshops under the same roof as Fabergé at the headquarters in Bolshaya Morskaya Street, so Fabergé himself was able to supervise some of the work. The workmasters, whose 'craft and ingenuity' is described by Bainbridge as being of the same artistic standard as that of the designers, must have had some influence on the design of the objects they were expected to execute. This is borne out by the fact that the three head workmasters each have a recognizable personal style. Erik Kollin, for example, worked mostly with gold in the antique style of the Kerch jewellery. Michael Perchin, who followed as head workmaster in 1886, can be recognized by the Louis XV or rococo style. Henrik Wigström, who succeeded in 1903, worked mostly in the classical styles of Louis XVI and the Empire. It must not be forgotten that Wigström's period as head workmaster was also the one in which the majority of objects we know as Fabergé were produced.

Finally, when the object was ready to be packed (generally in a box made of maple or holly and with a silk lining stamped with the firm's logo), Fabergé himself made the decision whether or not it should be labelled as a 'Fabergé'. Many times Bainbridge recalls having

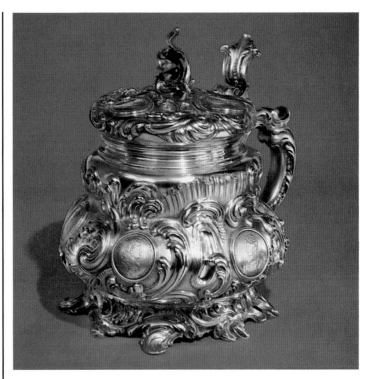

Massive silver tankard in the Louis XV rococo style set with 18th century rouble coins. 27.3 cm (10¾ inches) high

seen Fabergé reject, without comment, an article which did not please him. As had been stated in the 1899 catalogue, 'each item − even if the value is not higher than one rouble − is fabricated with precision in all details'. An item which did not conform to these high standards was probably returned to the workshop to be remodelled or dismantled, even if not destroyed, as tradition has it, by the hammer of the Master himself.

Whether Fabergé did actually examine and pass judgement on all the items produced in the workshops seems questionable. By 1900 there was a huge demand for his work. The total number

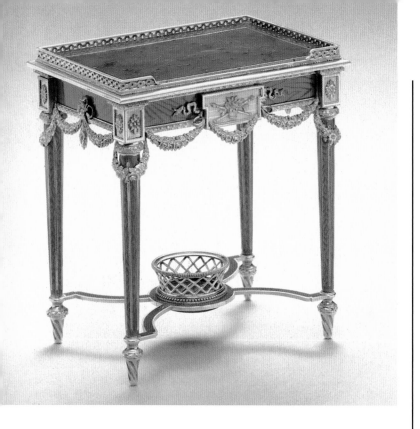

Above: Miniature bonbonnière in the
shape of a Louis XVI style table.
Varicoloured gold with white and mahogany coloured enamel 8.9 cm (3½ inches)

imprint or cachet. This was probably
due as much to his imposing, patriarchal
personality as to the administrative
skills with which he supervised the
artists. Fabergé had an extraordinary
ability to find the artist he needed to
meet his high standards. The appointment of head workmasters was of
course an effective way of delegating
his controlling powers – powers which
later devolved upon his sons, and
especially upon Eugène.

Even though many pieces are imita-
tive in style, drawing upon the entire
vocabulary of historical ornament,
Fabergé cannot be accused of plagiar-
ism. He never copied to the extent
of producing an exact replica. Always

of objects produced has been estimated
at about 120,000, and many designs
were produced in large numbers. Although Fabergé's objects were never
mass-produced, the multiplication of
certain types was permissible. As Bainbridge stated, 'with the ever-growing
demand on his inventive skill for something new, colour (of the enamel)
became of supreme importance. A
change of colour meant a new article'.
It seems unlikely that Fabergé checked
all these 'new articles' himself.

In view of the diversity of influences
on style, design and workmanship it is
astonishing that each piece carries so
recognizably Fabergé's own stylistic

Below: Silver-gilt and enamel picture
frame in the neo-classical style, signed with
the Imperial warrant mark of Fabergé
Moscow. 13.3 cm (5¼ inches) high

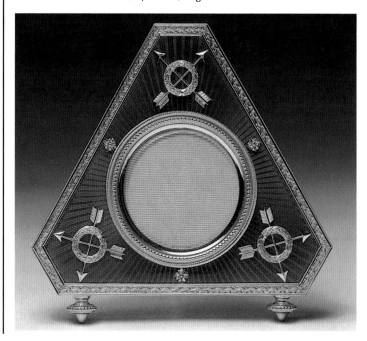

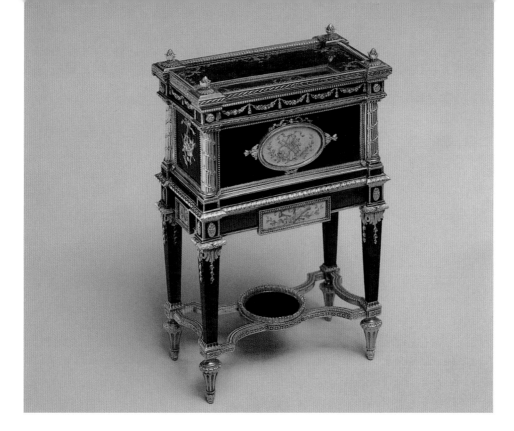

Miniature replica of a secretaire *in Louis XVI style, of varicoloured gold and agate with enamel plaques. 13.3 cm (5¼ inches)*

some detail, however minute, was changed or adapted to make the work look more pleasing to the modern eye. His designs are usually new interpretations of past styles. As Bainbridge says, the typical Fabergé style, which had already been recognized and acclaimed by the French goldsmiths at the World Exhibition in Paris in 1900, is the one which develops the classical French style. The simplicity of the classical Louis XVI and Empire styles reached new heights in Fabergé's art and is the source of its elegance.

Not all Fabergé's objects have escaped aesthetic disapproval. One group, arguably bizarre or eccentric in style, has been categorized as kitsch or *mauvais goût*. It could equally be argued that Fabergé's influence has transmutted them, in design, or execution, or material, into objects of artistic value. Fabergé's ability to transcend the banal is an important part of his style.

One other important aspect of Fabergé's art should be mentioned: his objects need to be touched and handled to reveal the supreme skill that has been brought to the work. Most pieces have the quality of being artistic toys, pleasing to touch and turn in the hands. We may quote from the art critic René Chanteclair with his comment (published in 1900) on the heart suprise of the 1899 Imperial Pansy Egg: 'The idea of this *bibelot* is charming, the mechanism ingenious, but like most of the other pieces it has more the character and appearance of a toy than of an *objet d'art*'.

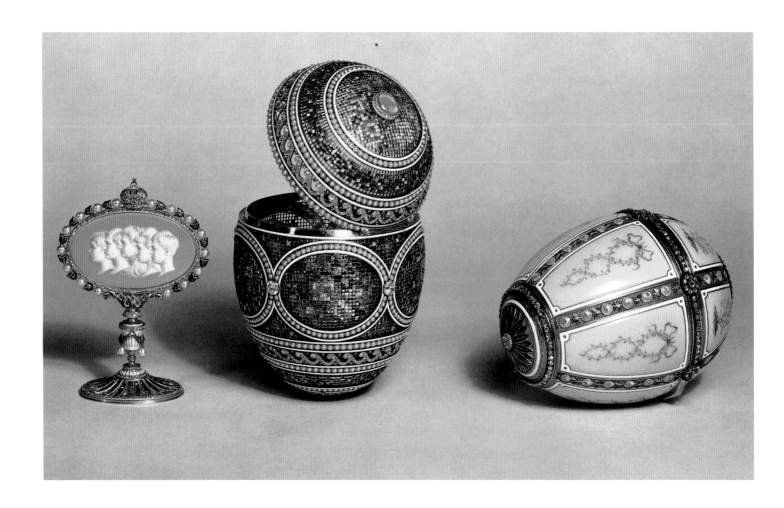

Left and centre: *The Mosaic Easter*
Egg. Its surprise shows the miniature
portraits of the five Imperial children.
9.2 cm (3⅝ inches) high
Right: *Easter egg with enamelled panels*
presented by Alexander Kelch to his wife
Barbara in 1899. 8.9 cm (3½ inches) high.
(English Royal Collection)

Chapter Two

IMPERIAL EASTER EGGS

The Imperial Easter Eggs – exquisite artifacts of jewels and precious metals – are Fabergé's finest and most famous achievement. Between 1885 and 1916 some 54 of these amazing objects were commissioned by the Tsars Alexander III and Nicholas II as Easter presents for the Tsarinas Marie and Alexandra Feodorovna: 47 are known to exist. Each, together with the cunningly wrought 'surprise' which was frequently concealed inside, is a masterpiece of elegance, inventiveness, ingenuity and craftsmanship. They reflect the wealth and extravagance as well as the taste and interests of the Russian Imperial court, and have been described as the last blossoming of European art in the service of great patrons.

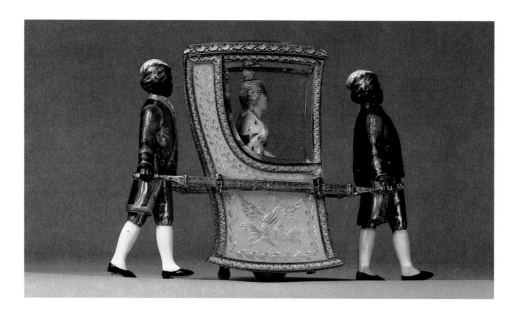

Sedan chair with a figure of Catherine the Great carried by two blackamoors; the surprise of the 1914 Imperial Easter Egg. Workmaster, Henrik Wigström. 7 cm (2¾ inches) high

He (Tsar Nicholas II) wrote me a most charming letter and presented me with a most beautiful Easter egg. Fabergé brought it to me himself. It is a true *chef-d'oeuvre*, in pink enamel and inside a *porte-chaise* carried by two negroes with Empress Catherine in it wearing a little crown on her head. You wind it up and then the negroes walk: it is an unbelievably beautiful and superbly fine piece of work. Fabergé is the greatest genius of our time, I also told him: *Vous êtes un génie incomparable.*

The pink enamel Easter egg described by the Empress Marie Feodorovna in a letter dated 8 April 1914 is the one with pink panels painted *en grisaille* with symbols of the arts. Called the Grisaille or Catherine the Great Egg, it is now in the Hillwood Museum, Washington, D.C. It also bears the date 1914 and the monogram of the Empress under portrait diamonds.

The letter by the Dowager Empress illustrates her enthusiasm for Fabergé and his work and also gives an idea of how close Fabergé was to the Imperial family. He himself delivered the Easter present from the Tsar, who was at the time on his estate in Livadia in the Crimea. It had become a tradition for Fabergé to hand over the Easter egg to the Empress himself ever since he had created the first of the series in 1885.

First Imperial Egg

It was Alexander III who had asked Fabergé to make an egg for Easter 1885 as a present for the Tsarina. The story goes that the Tsar wished to give his wife, who was born a Danish princess, a very special Easter present to remind her of her Danish home. Fabergé's first Imperial Easter egg was a copy of a similar egg, made of gold and opaque white enamel and containing a miniature hen, which is still today in the Danish royal collection at Rosenborg Castle in Copenhagen. The immediate success of this idea resulted in an Imperial commission for a new Fabergé egg every year: and there followed the extraordinary series of 54 Imperial presentation Easter eggs.

There has been much discussion about the total number of Easter eggs, their dating and their present whereabouts. Although some recently published works have established some facts about the first eggs to be commissioned, the task of establishing a definitive list of eggs seems to be impossible. Marina Lopato of the Hermitage Museum, Leningrad, (in her article 'Fresh Light on Carl Fabergé' in *Apollo* CXIX, January 1984) has given a translation of the dossier of the Imperial cabinet. This has established the date of the creation of the first Imperial Easter egg (which is now in the Forbes collection) as 1885. The egg was described as 'made of white enamel with a crown decorated with rubies, brilliants and rose diamonds'. The absence of a reference to the hen may, according to Lopato, be due to the brevity of the descriptions in the file, which dates from 1889. Apart from this first egg, only one of six other eggs recorded in the list is known – the Serpent Clock Egg of 1887 (also in the Forbes Collection). Together with the other eggs, which were previously ascribed to the period of the reign of Alexander III, there would have been 14 eggs made for only ten Easter occasions. The additional four eggs were probably given to members of the Imperial family other than the Empress. Géza von Habsburg suggested in the catalogue of the Munich exhibition of 1987) that they were perhaps given to the Tsarevich.

In spite of such unresolved questions the main facts seem clear enough. Between 1885 and his death in 1894 Alexander III gave his wife, the Empress Marie Feodorovna, ten Easter eggs. Their son, Tsar Nicholas II, continued the tradition, giving lavish Easter pre-

The first Imperial Easter Egg, 1885, and its surprise, a gold hen (Forbes Collection)

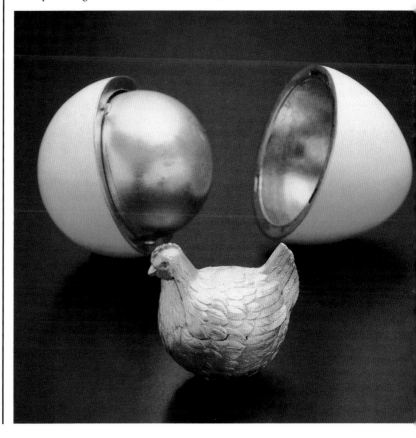

sents not only to his wife, the Empress Alexandra Feodorovna, but also to his mother. From 1895 until 1916 each empress received 22 eggs. Whether eggs were made and delivered for Easter 1917 has not been conclusively demonstrated. The total number of the series of Imperial eggs must therefore have been 54, or 56 if eggs for 1917 are included.

Of the 47 that are known to exist, ten are kept in the Kremlin in Moscow and eleven are in the Forbes Collection, New York. There are 16 in American collections and a further eight in private European collections. The location of two eggs is unknown and they are recorded only in photographs.

All the Easter eggs are highly miniaturized, lavish products reflecting the the splendour of the Imperial court. They constitute the last blossoming of European art in the service of great patrons. Fabergé did not allow himself to make any repetitions when working on these most important commissions and each of these masterpieces is an attempt to surpass its predecessor in invention, beauty and elegance.

The idea of the Easter present in the form of an egg implied that it should contain a surprise. Traditionally small jewels and miniature Easter eggs were concealed in these presents. The first and the second Imperial Easter eggs apparently contained a ruby and a sapphire egg-shaped pendant as surprises.

Later, Fabergé seems to have concentrated increasingly on the invention of unusual Easter egg surprises. Miniature portraits of members of the Imperial

Imperial Easter Egg presented to the Dowager Empress Marie by Nicholas II in 1895. The surprise is a folding screen of miniatures showing Danish and Russian palaces and the Imperial yachts. The egg is 10.2 cm (4 inches) high

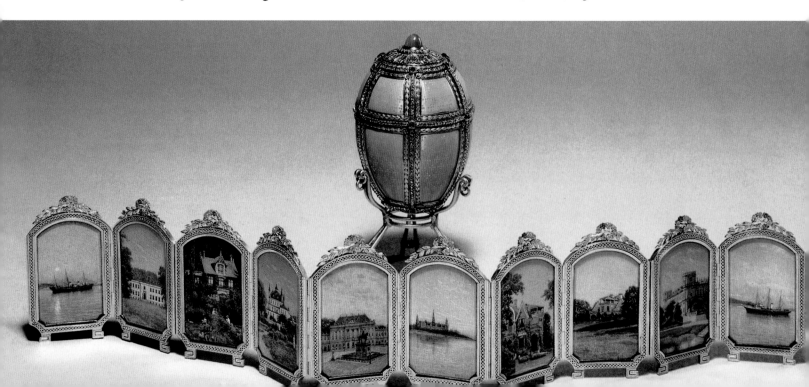

family in elaborate frames were often enclosed, as were miniatures painted with views of Imperial residences and palaces. Two eggs open to reveal miniature models of palaces inside: the Gatchina Palace, a residence of the Dowager Empress near St Petersburg, is the surprise of the Easter egg which was probably made in 1901. The Easter egg given in 1908 to Empress Alexandra Feodorovna conceals a model of the Alexander Palace, the residence of the Tsar's family in Tsarskoe Selo.

Monuments, such as the statue of Peter the Great by Falconet or the one of Alexander III by Trubetzkoi, were copied in miniature (1903 and 1910); so were the cruiser *Pamyat Azova*, on which Nicholas II had toured the world, and the Imperial yacht *Standart* (1891 and 1909).

The creation of the surprise for the 1897 Coronation Easter egg is well documented. It was a miniature replica, in gold and enamel, of the Imperial coach used in 1896 for the Coronation of Nicholas II and Empress Alexandra in Moscow. Details were faithfully copied from the original and include engraved rock crystal windows as well as the two steps which are let down when the doors are opened. This model was made by George Stein, who was first master carriage-builder and then an engraver with Fabergé, and who was known for his precise hand and his eye for the minutest detail. He spent about fifteen months working on this model.

Although the egg itself is signed by the chief workmaster Michael Perchin, Henrik Wigström, his assistant (and from 1903 his successor) was involved in the manufacture of this surprise, supervising the enamelling. Wigström's daughter recalled going with her father

The Trans-Siberian Railway Egg of 1900 (Armoury Museum, The Kremlin, Moscow)

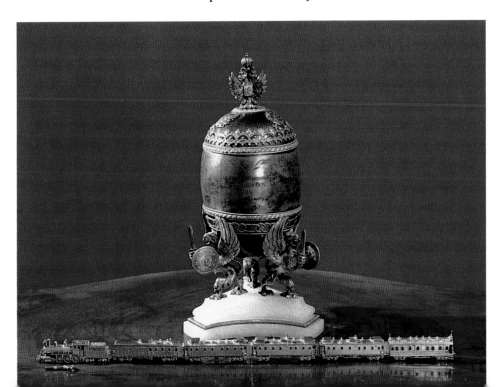

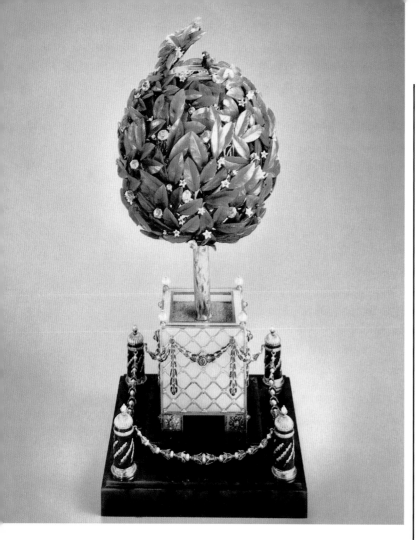

to the Imperial stables to check the exact colour on the seat of the Coronation coach. As the model was about to be enamelled he needed to find just the right shades of 'raspberry red'.

A similar toy-like miniature replica is the surprise of the 1900 egg with the Trans-Siberian express. This is a train composed of engine, tender, and five coaches, and includes such minute detail as the Imperial chapel and even inscriptions for 'smokers' or 'ladies only' compartments. This egg with its surprise had been seen and admired when exhibited in St Petersburg in 1902. Each coach of the train is connec-

ted to the next one by a hinge, and they can be folded together like a penknife to fit snugly into the shell of the egg.

The automata are a special category of Easter egg surprises. They seemed to have appealed especially to Fabergé's inventiveness. There are six Easter eggs known to have automata as surprises, not to mention the more or less elaborate egg-shaped clocks: the 1900 Cuckoo Egg, 1906 Swan Egg, 1908 Peacock Egg, 1911 Orange Tree Egg and the Kelch Pine Cone and Chanticleer Eggs.

The so-called Cuckoo Egg, whose surprise is in fact not a cuckoo but a cockerel, is in the shape of a clock decorated in an original style blending baroque and moorish elements. The surprise is a singing-bird mechanism which is independent of the clock movement. The bird automaton is released by pushing a button; the open-work cover on the top of the egg lifts to reveal a cockerel decorated with natural coloured feathers. Like the bird automata of early 19th century Swiss origin, the cock opens its beak and moves its wings rhythmically, while the sound of a singing bird can be heard. This sound is produced by a bellows.

The singing-bird automaton of the 1911 Orange Tree Egg is similar, but a highly sophisticated mechanism was

Above: *The Orange Tree Egg, 1911. The top opens to reveal a singing bird. 26.7 cm (10½ inches). (Forbes Collection)*
Opposite: *The Cuckoo Clock Egg; the surprise is a cockerel. Shown actual size. (Forbes Collection)*

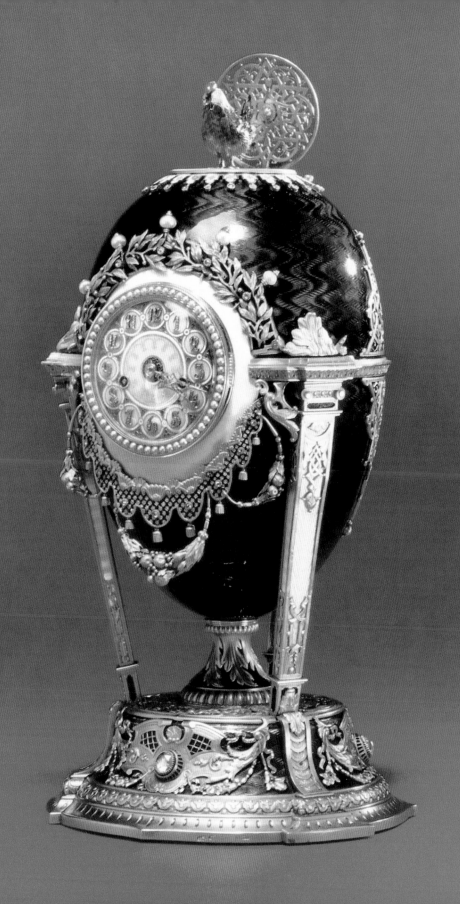

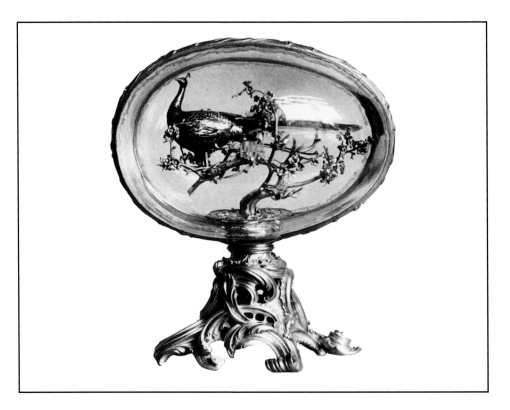

used for the surprise in the 1906 Swan Egg. This is a swan swimming on a miniature lake made of aquamarine with applied gold waterlilies which has a wind-up mechanism concealed under one wing. When this is operated the swan, which is less than 5 cm (2 inches) long, starts to glide along, moving its webbed feet. It wags its tail characteristically and the head and arched neck are proudly raised and then lowered. The wings open and spread to display each set of feathers separately.

A similar bird automaton is the surprise of the 1908 Peacock Egg, which was obviously inspired by the famous peacock automaton by James Cox in the Hermitage. When it is wound up and placed on a flat surface this enamelled gold bird struts proudly about, placing

The Peacock Egg, presented to the Dowager Empress in 1908. 15.2 cm (6 inches) high. Original Fabergé photograph

one leg carefully before the other, moving its head and, at intervals, spreading and closing its colourful tail. The workmaster Dorofeev, a self-taught mechanic, is said to have worked on this automaton for three years.

Another automaton is the one described in the Empress Marie Feodorovna's letter. It is the Sedan Chair with the Empress Catherine the Great, the surprise of the 1914 Easter egg. The sedan chair is carried by two court lackeys. The Empress is realistically represented, wearing a crown and ermine-trimmed Imperial robes, enamelled in translucent colours. The sedan chair, with its rock crystal windows, is chased and engraved in vari-coloured gold and decorated with the Imperial eagle. The moors who carry the chair are dressed in red enamelled liveries and wear turbans. When the clockwork mechanism is wound up the two lackeys start to walk, slowly moving their legs while the chair is pushed by two tiny wheels connected to the mechanism.

It was made in the workshop of Henrik Wigström and bears the signature 'FABERGE' in Latin characters. inspiration for this amusing object apparently derives from a similar automaton sedan chair, dating from the 18th century, which is in the collection at the Hermitage.

In 1885, when Alexander III had asked Fabergé to create an Easter present, the tradition of exchanging Easter gifts in the form of an egg was well established in Russia. Easter eggs were considered symbols representing the resurrection of Christ, and therefore, symbols of life itself. A few years before, in the late 1870s, an egg enclosing an icon of the Virgin Vladimirskaya had been made for Tsar Alexander II by the St Petersburg goldsmith Joseph Nordberg. The icon and the support, composed of orthodox crosses, emphasize the religious character of the egg (now in the Forbes Collection, New York).

Fabergé was able to look back in art history to find a number of examples of egg-shaped objects which served him as artistic sources.

There were eggs in the Imperial collections which would have been known to Fabergé and which may still be seen in the treasury of the Hermitage. One is an egg-shaped incense-burner of gold and pale purple enamel decorated with a grisaille painting glorifying Catherine the Great. It is recorded as the work of the goldsmith Jean-Jacques Duc and dates from about 1780. Also in the Hermitage is a set of four egg-shaped vodka beakers with covers, openwork gold mounts and turned ivory feet. They were used by Fabergé as the prototype for the Blue Enamel Ribbed Egg, now in the Niarchos Collection.

For the 1903 Peter the Great Egg Fabergé took his inspiration from an egg-shaped jewelled gold *nécessaire* containing a watch, which was made in Paris in 1757 and came to St Petersburg as a present for Empress Elizabeth (1741–1761).

Another well-known stylistic inspiration for one of Fabergé's eggs is the elliptical gold-mounted chalcedony *nécessaire* from the Green Vaults in Dresden which has traditionally been ascribed to the goldsmith, Le Roy. Its French Regency style, dating from around 1720, was copied by Fabergé in the so-called Renaissance Egg of 1894 (Forbes Collection). As the original and copy differ in shape and in the decor-

Overleaf, left: The Lilies-of-the-Valley Egg, dated 5 April 1899. The surprise consists of the miniature portraits of the Tsar and the Grand Duchesses Olga and Tatiana. (Forbes Collection, New York)
Right: *The Grisaille or Catherine the Great Egg, 1914*

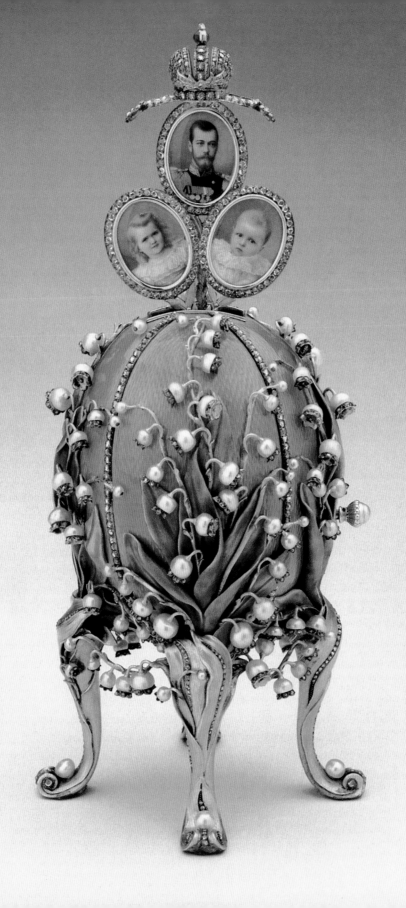

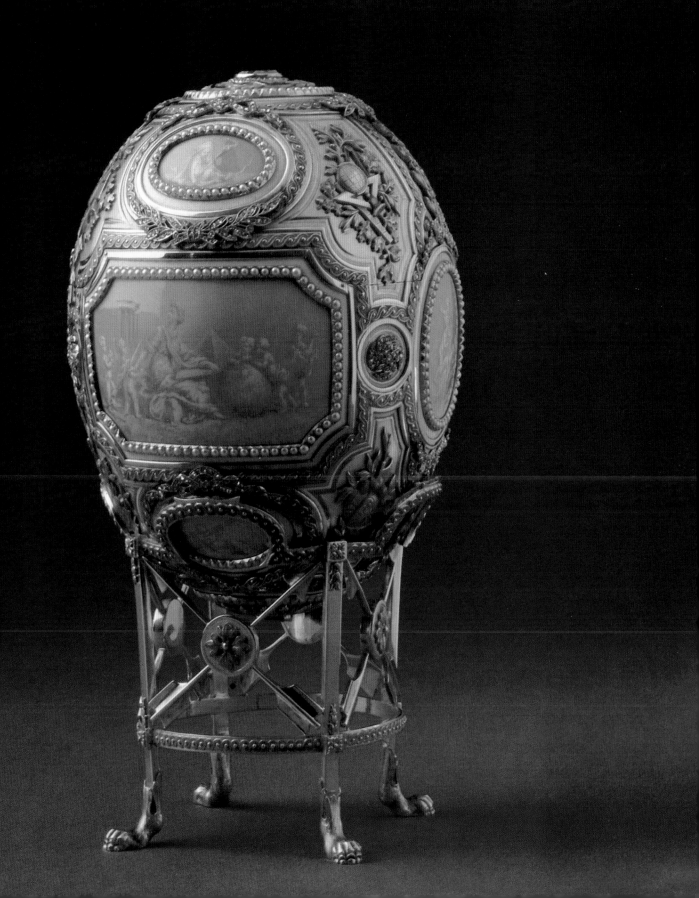

ation of the interior, it has been suggested that the design of Fabergé's egg may have been derived from a mid-19th century colour print rather than from the Dresden original.

It can, however, be said of all the Fabergé eggs that follow earlier styles or originals that none of them is, in fact, an exact copy or an actual imitation. Fabergé used the original work of art only as a source of inspiration. To each of his creations he gave his own distinctive cachet – reshaping, for example, the elliptical Le Roy casket, or varying the proportions of the decoration.

This aspect of the Fabergé cachet was criticized by some of his contempories. Chanteclair, for instance, refers in his article on the 1900 Paris International Exhibition to the 1891 Pamyat Azova Egg:

This small object, made by Holmström represents one year's work: we did not greatly admire the patina, the external ornaments of the egg, which are slightly exaggerated in the combination of colours, and the rose-cut diamonds in the centres of the rococo scrolls. As Monsieur Fabergé remains a true admirer of the French styles, we think he could have easily chosen among each of these some ornamentations which are less known, but equally decorative.

Clearly Fabergé had not intended to make a true copy of an 18th century piece, but an object in his personal style inspired by an historical item.

There are undoubtedly other egg-shaped pieces of earlier periods which could be seen as direct sources for the designs of Fabergé's Imperial eggs. Many of them freely adapt or combine historical styles, such as the Louis XV style with its bold rococo scrolls or the Louis XVI style with flower garlands and bows. Some are representative of the art nouveau movement which became popular in the last decade of the 19th century; the 1898 Lilies-of-the-Valley Egg and the 1899 Pansy Egg are typical examples of this style, which took some of its artistic inspiration from flowers and plants.

But Fabergé's masterpieces, such as the 1897 Coronation Egg, the Mosaic and the Winter Egg were very much his own invention. They are specifically *Fabergé*. They do not follow the normal sources of inspiration recognized by his contemporaries.

1914 Mosaic Egg

The 1914 Mosaic Egg, which consists of a gold mounted platinum network partially pavé-set with diamonds and coloured gems, has five oval panels decorated with flower motifs in a mosaic-like technique. It was designed by Alma Klee, the daughter of the Fabergé workmaster Knut Oskar Pihl. She had the inspiration for this very unusual and delicate decoration for an egg when seeing her mother-in-law's *petit point* embroidery. The mosaic

Opposite: The Coronation Egg, dated 1897, with its surprise, an exact replica of the coronation coach. (Forbes Collection)

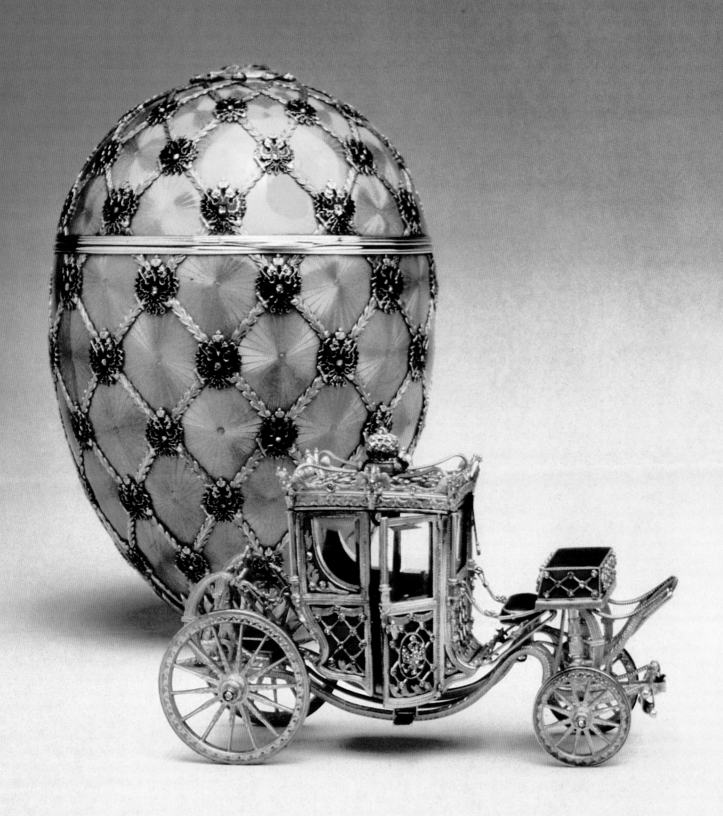

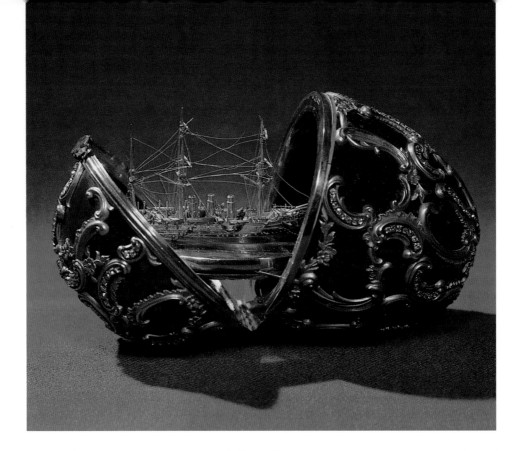

Imperial Easter egg containing a model of the cruiser, Pamyat Azova, dated 1891. (Armoury Museum, The Kremlin, Moscow)

network, which is also recorded in Holmström's stockbook as a design for a brooch, gives a pointillist effect. A very talented artist, Alma Klee also designed the 1913 Winter Egg which is decorated with diamond frost flowers.

After the outbreak of war the eggs made for Easter in 1915 and 1916 were much simpler in style and decoration. They are characterized by the Red Cross theme and have no embellishments of diamonds or pearls. Silver rather than gold was used as the ground for the enamelling.

The Easter present for Empress Alexandra in 1916 was an egg made of steel supported by four artillery shells.

The surprise is a miniature painting of the Tsar reviewing troops at the front (Kremlin, Moscow). This and the 1916 Cross of St George Egg are the last eggs which can be said with certainty to have been made and delivered by Fabergé. Mystery surrounds the eggs made for Easter 1917: by then the Imperial family was already imprisoned. The eggs are said to have been made of Karelian birchwood and lapis lazuli, but whether they were ever completed or delivered is unknown.

Lost Eggs

It is fascinating to speculate on the possibility of discovering a lost or even unrecorded Imperial Easter Egg. Several eggs are in fact recorded as lost, although two of them are at least known from photographs. The Danish Jubilee

Egg, which has been given a new conjectural date of 1906 on stylistic and historical grounds, had been photographed by Fabergé and appears in an album of original photographs made for Fabergé's London branch. Its location was not even recorded in the article 'Russian Imperial Easter Gifts' by H C Bainbridge, which was published in *The Connoisseur* in 1934, nor has it since come to light.

The other egg of which only a photograph exists is the 1913 Winter Egg, which was sold at auction in 1949. Since then it has been recorded as part of the collection of Bryan Ledbrook Esq., but unfortunately it present whereabouts is unknown.

There are certainly some owners of Fabergé pieces who are unwilling that their possession of, for example, an Imperial Easter egg should become publicly known. This is perhaps understandable: the price paid, for example, by Malcolm Forbes for the 1900 Cuckoo Egg in 1985 was $1.76 million.

Mr Forbes has no hesitation in displaying his collection of Imperial eggs — they are on view at a special museum in the Forbes Building on Fifth Avenue in New York. Other owners, including the owner of the 1910 Egg with Love Trophies, are less keen.

The most recent rediscovery of an Imperial egg, the 1895 Rosebud Egg, has been vividly described by Christopher Forbes in the magazine April 1986 *Art & Antiques*:

The Rosebud Egg, for example, was purchased by Snowman from the

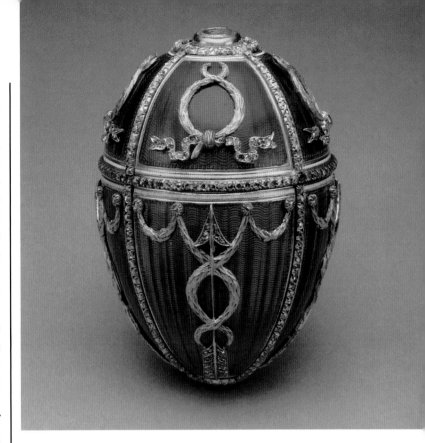

The Rosebud Egg, dated 1895. The shell opens to reveal its surprise, a yellow rosebud. (Forbes Collection)

Russian government auction in the 1920s. Back in London Snowman sold it to Charles Parson, who sold it to Henry Talbot de Vere Clifton; the egg then disappeared. (Rumour had it that Clifton has thrown it at his wife, the former Lillian Lowell).

One photograph of the egg survived in the Wartski archives, and was published in 1952. Subsequent editions of *The Art of Carl Fabergé* record it as 'present whereabouts unknown'. And so it was until a few months ago, when leading jewellery dealer Paul Vartanian heard a colleague say, casually, that a friend of his had a Fabergé egg: Would Paul like to see a snapshot? Good friend and neighbour that he is, Paul called me. After Byzantine negotiations I confirmed that it is the egg given by Nicholas II to his bride in 1895. (And yes, it has been damaged in a way that suggests it was either dropped . . . or thrown.)

The egg was subsequently acquired for the Forbes Collection where, having undergone a minor repair, it can now be admired in its original splendour.

Not infrequently, even when an Imperial Easter egg itself is recorded and preserved in a known collection, the surprise or part of the surprise associated with it may be lost. This is true even of the celebrated Coronation Egg. Its surprise, the model of the state carriage used by the Tsar and Empress at their coronation, is one of Fabergé's masterpieces in its own right. But according to the 1916 article in the Russian *Town and Country* magazine there was a further suprise: inside the carriage there was originally a small diamond egg – perhaps an egg-shaped briolette-cut diamond.

Another Easter egg surprise which has been separated from the original present was the 'sedan chair automaton carried by moors' that has been mentioned earlier. It belonged to the 1914 Catherine the Great (Grisaille) Egg. The egg was sold separately by the Soviet Government in about 1930 and the surprise came to the West in a similar way. The description of her 1914 Easter present from the Tsar, in the letter by the Empress Marie Feodo-

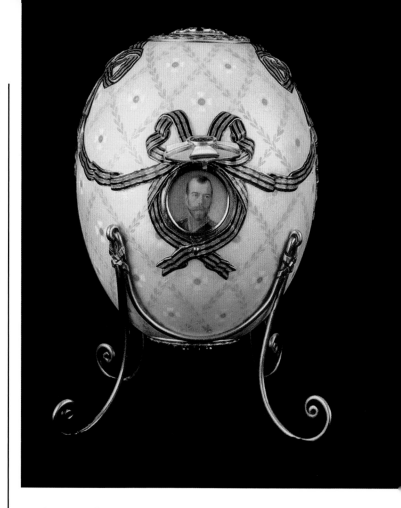

The Cross of St. George Egg, 1916. A medallion showing the St. George Cross lifts to reveal a portrait of Tsar Nicholas II

rovna, leaves no doubt about the historical connection. The egg itself now belongs to the Hillwood Collection, Washington D.C.

The sedan chair surprise came up for sale at auction in Geneva in 1985 as part of the collection of the late Sir Charles Clore where it fetched 1.43 million Swiss francs (about £500,000). This surprise and its egg are still apart.

The lavishness of the Imperial Easter eggs had already become famous during the last decade of the 19th century, although they were not publicly exhibited until the 1900 Exposition Universelle in Paris. It seems natural that other wealt y persons in Russia should have wished to follow the example of the Tsar by ordering similarly rich Easter presents.

The Siberian gold magnate and millionaire, Alexander Ferdinandovich Kelch, presented his wife Barbara with a series of eggs as sumptuous as those of the tsars. There are seven eggs known which were made for Kelch between 1898 and 1904. The first one, is quite appropriately a Hen Egg; the others are the 1899 Twelve-panel Egg, the 1900 Pine Cone Egg, the Apple Blossom Egg, the 1902 Rocaille Egg, the 1903 Bonbonnière Egg and the 1904 Chanticleer Egg.

Although for his Imperial patrons Faberge never produced two eggs even remotely alike he felt free to copy existing Imperial models of his own for other customers. This is the case with the Kelch Hen egg, which takes up the same idea as the first Imperial egg in a more developed form. Another example of this hen egg type appeared at an auction in Geneva in 1981. Its provenance was given as 'the estate of the late Maria Quisling', although the name of the person who originally commissioned the egg remains unknown. Details show that it was not a repetition of the Kelch egg: the Kelch Hen egg (Forbes Collection) opens into two halves lengthwise whereas the other divides crosswise. It was made by Michael Perchin sometime between 1899 and 1903. Unfortunately the egg had to be withdrawn from auction

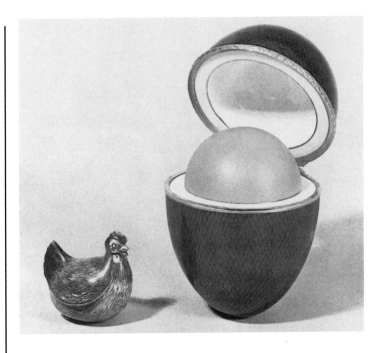

The Hen Egg from the Quisling Collection.
The shell is of strawberry red enamel

because of major damage to the enamel during the preview.

Fabergé also copied another Imperial egg for Kelch. This was the 1903 Kelch Bonbonnière Egg, which follows the style of the 1901 Gatchina Palace Egg with opalescent white enamel panels painted with Louis XVI ribbons and garlands. However, where the Imperial egg has pearl borders and table-cut diamonds as finials, the Kelch egg has the pearl bands decorated at intervals with emeralds and has moonstones instead of diamonds.

Another Russian client was Prince Youssoupoff, who acquired an egg of Imperial splendour, The Youssoupoff Egg was made in 1907 and has the shape of a table clock in the Louis XVI style. Originally it had three medallions con-

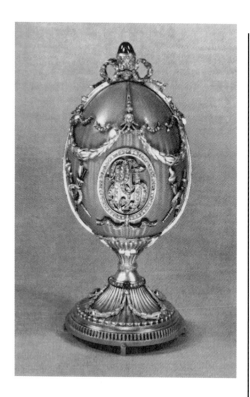

Jewelled, pink enamel egg by Hahn, one of Fabergé's competitors. 1895.
12.3 cm (4⅞ inches) high

taining portrait miniatures of Prince Felix Youssoupoff-Soumarokov-Elston and his two sons Nicholas and Felix. They have been replaced by the initials of the collector Maurice Y. Sandoz. The egg reverts to the scheme of the 1887 Serpent Clock Egg.

This same scheme was also followed in an egg acquired by the Duchess of Marlborough on her visit to St Petersburg in 1902. It was after an interval of nearly 15 years that Fabergé repeated the shape of the Imperial egg: but the original blue enamel colour was changed to pink, and it appears that the copy is larger than its prototype.

Some confusion in the dating of the Imperial eggs was caused by the series of Kelch eggs. Six of these had appeared on the art market in Paris in 1920 and were subsequently sold to collectors in the United States. They were catalogued at that time and it seems that they all had the same provenance, most of them bearing the initials BK for Barbara Kelch. Three of them, the Pine Cone, Apple Blossom and Chanticleer Eggs, were later given a false Imperial provenance, in the case of the Pine Cone Egg by the removal of the BK monogram. Dates ascribed to them were the dates of the lost Imperial eggs.

People have found the history of the eggs and their Imperial connection so fascinating that modern copies or fakes are provided with the trappings of Imperial provenance in the hope of increasing their value. The so-called Nicholas II Equestrian egg, which was to be sold at auction in New York in 1985, turned out to be a fake. It had supposedly been a present from the Empress Alexandra to the Tsar in 1913 and it had been recorded as such in many specialized studies. Although the shell of the egg had apparently been genuinely marked by Fabergé, it had received additions: a diamond-set Imperial eagle, a portrait of the Tsarina, and the equestrian statue of the Tsar after which the egg was named. But the embellishments with modern-cut diamonds were impossible for a genuine Fabergé object, and the provenance could never be proved. The egg had to be withdrawn from the sale and there followed a highly publicized lawsuit regarding its genuineness and value.

CATALOGUE OF EASTER EGGS

Presented by Tsar Alexander III to his wife, the Empress Marie Feodorovna:

1. The First Hen Egg, probable date 1885, unmarked. (Forbes Collection, New York)
2. The Resurrection Egg, probable date 1886. Workmaster M. Perchin. (Forbes Collection, New York)
3. Blue Enamel Ribbed Egg, possible date 1887. Workmaster M. Perchin. (Stavros Niarchos Collection, Paris)
4. The Serpent Clock Egg, possible date 1889. Workmaster M. Perchin. (Private collection, Switzerland)
5. The Spring Flowers Egg, possible date 1890. Workmaster M. Perchin. (Forbes Collection, New York)
6. The Pamyat Azova Egg, 1891. Workmaster M. Perchin. (Armoury Museum, The Kremlin, Moscow)
7. The Twelve-monogram Egg (The Silver Anniversary Egg), probable date 1892. Workmaster M. Perchin. (M. M. Post Collection: Hillwood Museum, Washington, D. C.)
8. The Caucasus Egg, dated 1893. Workmaster M. Perchin. (M. G. Gray Foundation Collection, New Orleans)
9. The Régence (Renaissance) Egg, dated 1894. Workmaster M. Perchin. (Forbes Collection, New York)

Spring Flowers Egg, late 19th century, in its original Fabergé case. (Forbes Collection)

These Easter eggs were made for Alexander III, according to Russian archives published by M. Lopato. **Present location is unknown:**

1886 Egg with Hen in a Basket
1888 Angel with an Egg in a Chariot
1888 Angel with a Clock in an Egg
1889 Pearl Egg
1890 Emerald Egg

Presented by Tsar Nicholas II to his mother, the Dowager Empress Marie Feodorovna:

10. The Danish Palace Egg, dated 1895. Workmaster M. Perchin. (M. G. Gray Foundation Collection, New Orleans)

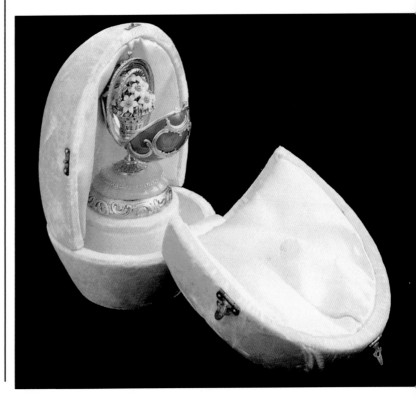

11. The Pelican Egg, dated 1897. Workmaster M. Perchin). (L. T. Pratt Collection: Virginia Museum of Fine Arts, Richmond)

12. The Lilies-of-the-Valley Egg, dated 1898. Workmaster M. Perchin. (Forbes Collection, New York)

13. The Pansy Egg, dated 1899. Workmaster M. Perchin. (Private collection, U.S.A.)

14. The Cuckoo Clock Egg, dated 1900. Workmaster M. Perchin. (Forbes Collection, New York)

15. The Gatchina Palace Egg, dated 1901. Workmaster M. Perchin. (The Walters Art Gallery, Baltimore)

16. The Alexander III Commemorative Egg, dated 1904. (Armoury Museum, The Kremlin, Moscow)

17. The Danish Jubilee Egg, probable date 1906. Lost.

18. The Peacock Egg, dated 1908. Workmaster H. Wigström. (Maurice Sandoz Collection, Musée de l'Horlogerie, Le Locle, Switzerland)

19. The Alexander III Equestrian Egg, dated 1910, signed Fabergé. (Armoury Museum, The Kremlin, Moscow)

20. The Orange Tree Egg, dated 1911. Signed Fabergé. (Forbes Collection, New York)

21. The Napoleonic Egg, dated 1912. Workmaster H. Wigström. (M. G., Gray Foundation Collection, New Orleans)

22. The Winter Egg, dated 1913. Lost

23. The Grisaille Egg, dated 1914. Workmaster H. Wigström. (M. M. Post Collection: Hillwood Museum, Washington D.C.)

24. The Red Cross Egg with Por-

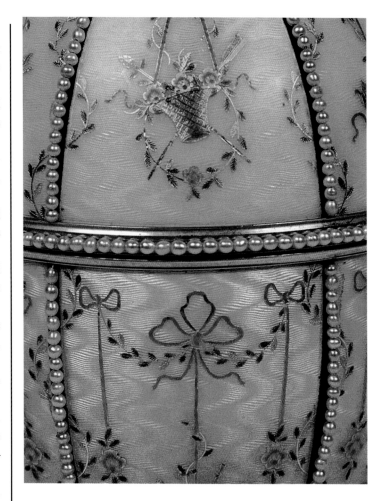

traits, dated 1915. Workmaster H. Wigström. (L. T. Pratt Collection: Virginia Museum of Fine Arts, Richmond)

25. The Cross of St. George Egg, dated 1916. Signed Fabergé. (Forbes Collection, New York)

Presented by Tsar Nicholas II to his wife, the Empress Alexandra Feodorovna:

26. The Rosebud Egg, dated 1895. Workmaster M. Perchin. (Forbes Collection, New York)

27. The Egg with Revolving Miniatures, probable date 1896. Workmaster

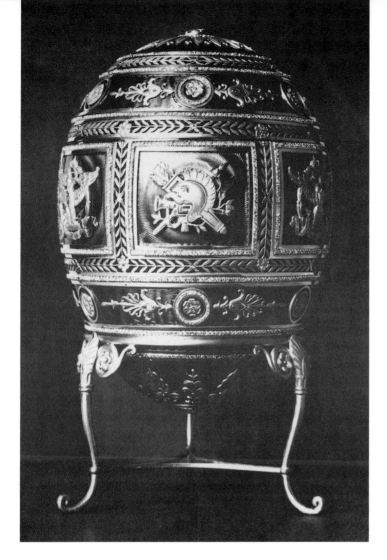

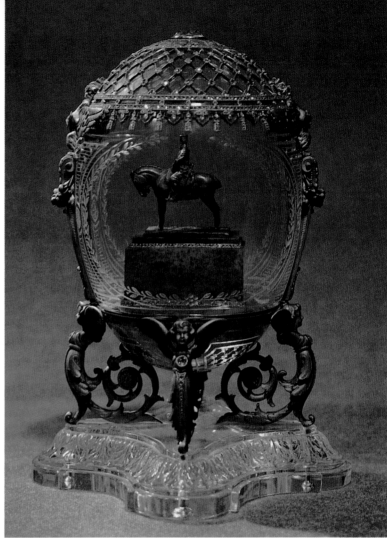

M. Perchin. (L. T. Pratt Collection: Virginia Museum of Fine Arts, Richmond)

28. The Coronation Egg, dated 1897. Workmaster M. Perchin. (Forbes Collection, New York)

29. The Madonna-Lily Egg, dated 1899. Workmaster M. Perchin. (Armoury Museum, the Kremlin, Moscow)

30. The Trans-Siberian Railway Egg, dated 1900. Workmaster M. Perchin. (Armoury Museum, Kremlin, Moscow)

31. The Clover Egg, dated 1902. Workmaster M. Perchin. (Armoury Museum, The Kremlin, Moscow)

***Opposite:** Detail from The Gatchina Palace Egg, dated 1901, showing the white guilloché enamel surface, painted with ribbons, garlands and classical emblems and inlaid with gold paillons. (Walters Art Gallery, Baltimore)*

***Left:** The Napoleonic Egg, 1912. Green enamel with Empire style gold Imperial eagles and military symbols. Original Fabergé photograph*

***Right:** The Alexander III Equestrian Egg, 1910 (Armoury Museum, The Kremlin, Moscow)*

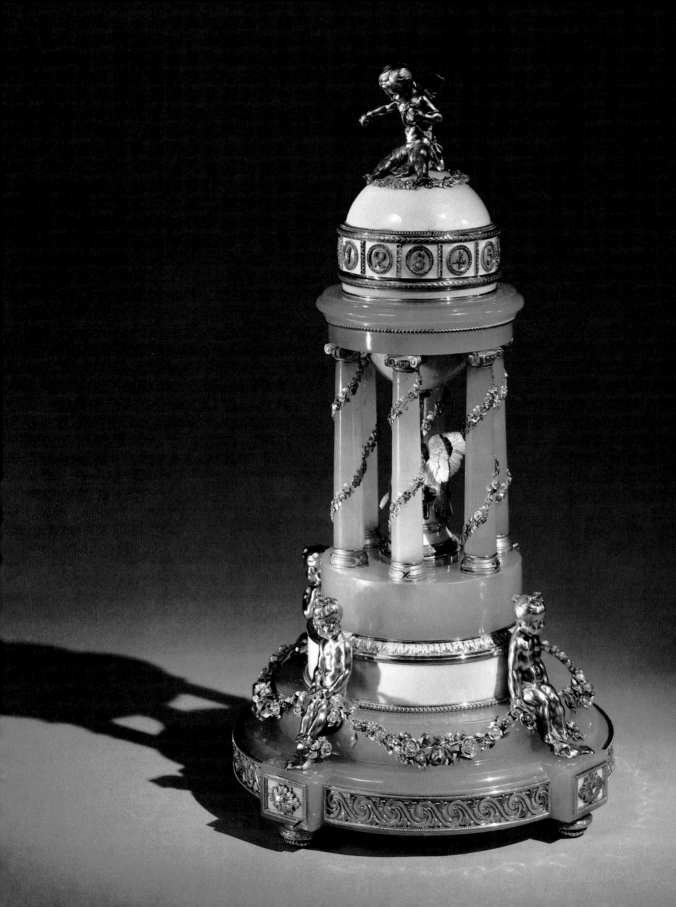

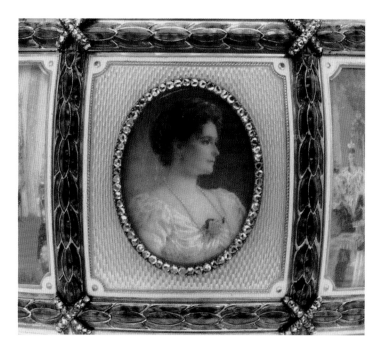
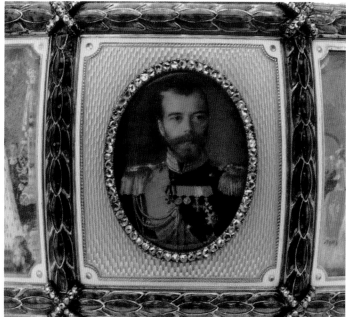

Opposite: The Colonnade Clock Egg. The cherub originally held an arrow pointing to the hour. 28.5 cm (11¼ inches) high (English Royal Collection)
Above: Details from the Fifteenth Anniversary Egg made to commemorate the anniversary of the Tsar's accession, dated 1911. The portraits of the Empress and the Tsar Nicholas II are by Vassily Zuiev.

32. The Peter the Great Egg, dated 1903. Workmaster M. Perchin. (L. T. Pratt Collection: Virginia Museum of Fine Arts, Richmond)
33. The Uspensky Cathedral Egg, dated 1904, signed Fabergé. (Armoury Museum, The Kremlin, Moscow)
34. The Colonnade Clock Egg, probable date 1905. Workmaster H. Wigström. (English Royal Collection)
35. The Swan Egg, dated 1906. (Maurice Sandoz Collection, Musee de l'Horlogerie, Le Locle, Switzerland)

36. The Rose Trellis Egg, dated 1907. (The Walters Art Gallery, Baltimore)
37. The Alexander Palace Egg, dated 1908. Workmaster H. Wigström. (Armoury Museum, The Kremlin, Moscow)
38. The Standart Egg, probable date 1909. Workmaster H. Wigström. (Armoury Museum, The Kremlin, Moscow)
39. The Love Trophy Egg, probable date 1910. (Private collection, U.S.A.)
40. The Fifteenth Anniversary Egg, dated 1911. Signed Fabergé. (Forbes Collection, New York)
41. The Tsarevitch Egg, dated 1912. Workmaster H. Wigström. (L. T. Pratt Collection: Virginia Museum of Fine Arts, Richmond)
42. The Romanov Tercentenary Egg, dated 1913. Workmaster H. Wigström. (Armoury Museum, The Kremlin, Moscow)

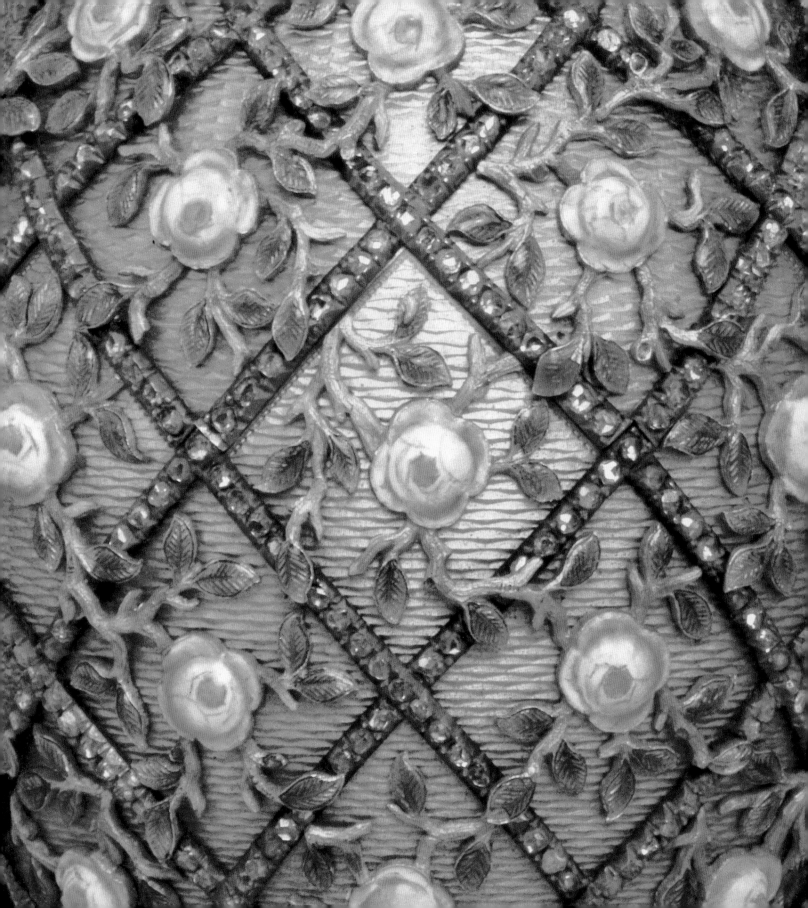

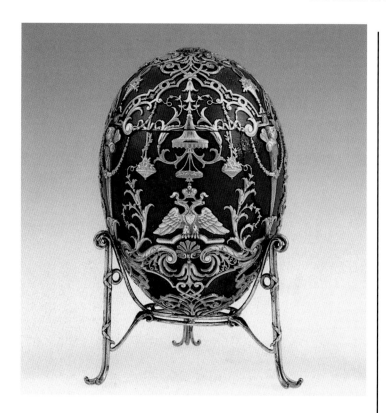

Opposite: Enlarged detail of The Rose Trellis Egg, dated 1907; it shows the intricate enamelwork of painted pink roses with emerald green leaves on a pale green guilloché ground within a diamond trellis. The egg is only 7.6 cm (3 inches) high
Above: *The Tsarevitch Egg, dated 1912. 12.1 cm (4¾ inches)*

43. The Mosaic Egg, dated 1914. Signed C. Fabergé. (English Royal Collection)

44. The Red Cross Egg with Resurrection Triptych, dated 1915. Workmaster H. Wigström. (I. E. Minshall Collection, The Cleveland Museum of Art, Cleveland)

45. The Steel Military Egg, dated 1916. Workmaster H. Wigström. (Armoury Museum, The Kremlin, Moscow)

The Kelch Eggs

46. The Hen Egg, dated 1898. Workmaster M. Perchin. (Forbes Collection, New York)

47. The Twelve-panel Egg, dated 1899. Workmaster M. Perchin. (Collection of Her Majesty the Queen)

48. The Pine Cone Egg, dated 1900. Workmaster M. Perchin. (Private collection U.S.A.)

49. The Apple Blossom Egg, probable date 1901. Workmaster M. Perchin. (Private collection U.S.A.)

50. The Rocaille Egg, dated 1902. Workmaster M. Perchin. (Private collection U.S.A.)

51. The Bonbonnière Egg, dated 1903. Workmaster M. Perchin. (Private collection U.S.A.)

52. The Chanticleer Egg, probable date 1904. Workmaster M. Perchin. (Forbes Collection, New York)

Other Eggs

53. Diamond Trellis Egg, late 19th century, Workmaster August Holmström. (Private collection, England)

54. The Duchess of Marlborough Egg, dated 1902, acquired in Russia by the American born Duchess, Consuelo Vanderbilt. Workmaster M. Perchin. (Forbes Collection, New York)

55. Hen Egg from the Quisling Collection, 1899–1903. Workmaster M. Perchin. (Present location unknown)

56. The Youssoupoff Easter Egg, dated 1907. Workmaster Henrik Wigström. (Maurice Sandoz Collection, Musée de l'Horlogerie, Le Locle, Switzerland)

57. The Nobel Ice Egg, circa 1914–1916. Lost.

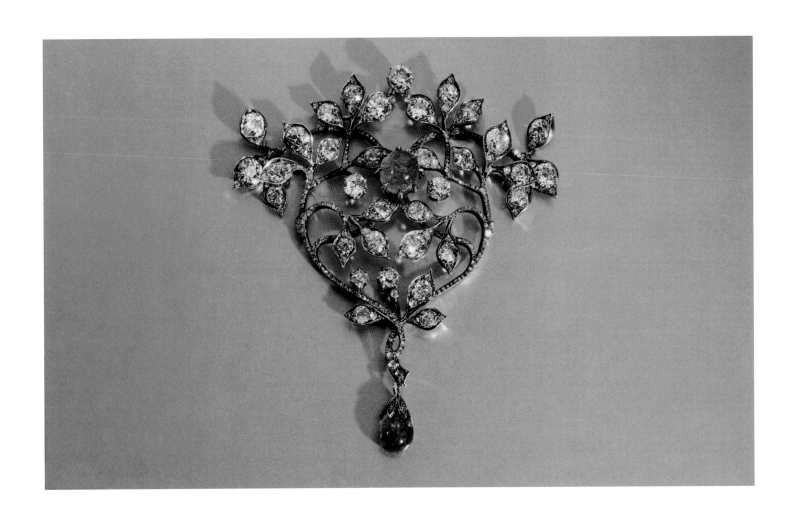

Diamond and Siberian emerald brooch in
the art nouveau style, made by Fabergé's
workshops in St Petersburg in about 1900

Chapter Three

JEWELLERY

Jewellery was the trade Fabergé was born to. He described himself as an 'artist-jeweller': and that, *par excellence*, is exactly what he was. In 1885 he received the warrant of 'Jeweller to the Imperial Court': the firm's output expanded rapidly, and he felt free to innovate. He re-introduced colour to jewellery – rubies, sapphires, emeralds, semiprecious stones, enamel – and revived the use of rose-cut diamonds. New motifs, such as ice and frost crystals, were devised. And the carved, miniature egg-shaped pendants, in enormous variety, for which Fabergé is renowned, became *le dernier cri* with his fashionable clientèle.

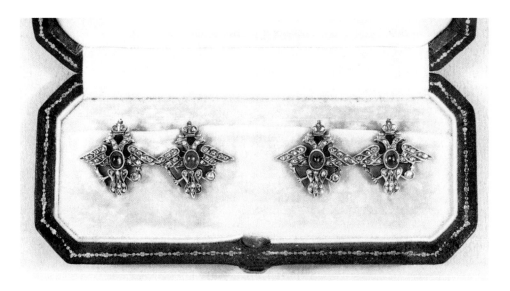

Imperial presentation cuff-links, set with diamonds and cabochon sapphires, in their original case. Workmaster, August Hollming, circa 1910

Fabergé regarded himself as an artist-jeweller and always emphasized the artistic side of the objects he made with precious stones. Indeed the success of his firm was based on the revolutionary idea of transforming items of jewellery into *objets d'art* whose aesthetic worth was not directly related to the value of the material involved.

It was a time when jewels were made of heavy, polished gold studded with large brilliant-cut diamonds just for the visual effect of richness. This was certainly the fashion around 1870 in Europe, and especially in Russia. Fabergé brought something completely new: he introduced colour into jewellery. This was not just the use of coloured stones such as rubies, sapphires or emeralds (which anyway he preferred in the shape of cabochons for their more subtle sparkle); he also used semiprecious stones in combination with diamonds – moonstones in particular – and a variety of decorative hardstones which were often regarded by other jewellers as cheap and unsuitable for use in important jewellery. Another way of combining jewels with colour was the use of enamel, which is particularly effective in small decorative pieces.

Such items were typical of the firm's output and form one of the pillars upon which Fabergé's fame rests. But the larger pieces of jewellery, made exclusively of precious stones, also played a part.

Important Jewellery

The firm of Fabergé made itself known as 'Jewellers to the Imperial Court' and consequently received many orders for large parures of diamonds and coloured stones. To meet the demand Fabergé always kept tiaras, necklaces, bracelets and brooches in stock.

At the 1900 Paris World Fair he exhibited a tiara 'in the Muscovite style, all in diamonds with ornaments of Byzantine inspiration' which was particularly commended by the adjudicators for the remarkable execution of the work, especially of the stone setting. It was their opinion that in his work 'the extreme limits of perfection are reached'. It has also to be said that Fabergé, himself a great specialist in the field of gemmology, always used the best stones he could find. Not surprisingly, he was commissioned by the Imperial court to make larger items of jewellery. There was a large emerald and pearl necklace made in the 17th century Russian style for the Imperial costume ball in 1898; a tiara with diamonds and turquoises; a brooch in the shape of a rose made with large diamonds from the Imperial treasury; and a triangular stomacher of diamonds and cabochon emeralds, the largest weighing 45 carats. The stomacher was commissioned by Grand Duchess Elisabeth Feodorovna in 1900 and was made by the Moscow workshop. These pieces are recorded in the inventory of the Imperial jewels drawn up in the 1920s, after the Russian Revolution, with the help of Fabergé's son Agathon, who was one of the top experts on precious stones at the time. In London in 1914 Fabergé had sold to Mrs Wrohan a diamond tiara for the then extremely high price of £1,400. It was an item from stock.

Stylistically most of these pieces follow the classical lines of the time, with either flower motifs or garlands and bows, usually set with diamonds. An

Diamond necklace, signed by August Hollming, in its original fitted case, circa 1900

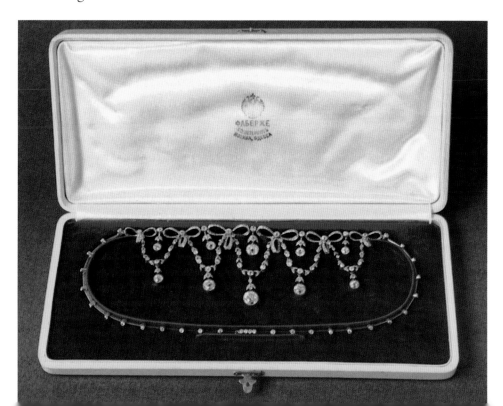

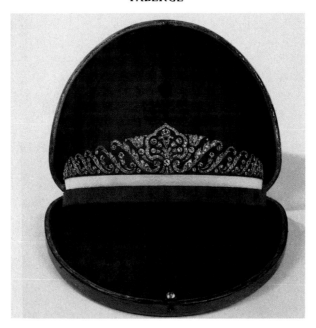

Diamond tiara with pale blue guilloché enamel bandeau, in its original fitted case

example is the diamond necklace made for the Russo-Finnish brewing magnate Sinebrikov, which is now in the Forbes Collection. It is interesting that there are some outstanding pieces of jewellery in the art nouveau style – a tiara decorated with cyclamen from Holmström's workshop, a brooch in the shape of a tree set with cabochon Siberian emeralds.

Most of the larger pieces of jewellery did not survive the years following the Russian Revolution. They were broken up and sold by the Russian emigrants for the value of the stones. It was not just that these jewels were more or less classical in style and therefore hard to identify as Fabergé jewellery: many went unrecognised, especially those mounted in platinum, because they had no markings.

Principal jewellers in the firm were August Holmström (1829–1903), who had a large workshop in St. Petersburg, and Knut Oskar Pihl (1860–1897), who worked in Moscow from 1887 on. Holmström had worked previously for Gustav Fabergé and was later given responsibility for the firm's jewellery production. His daughter Fanny married Pihl and their daughter Alma Teresia is known for her jewellery designs. The sons of both Holmström and Pihl continued their father's workshops, Albert Holmström (1876–1925) in St Petersburg and Oskar Woldemar Pihl (1890–1959) in Moscow. The chief jewellers were assisted by other master jewellers who also did work for other workshops specializing in *objets d'art*, enamel and hardstones.

Rosecut Diamonds

One thing that is typical of Fabergé work in general, whether jewellery or objects, is the profuse application of rose-cut diamonds. In this Fabergé was following a tradition peculiar to the Russian jeweller. From about 1750 onwards it had been the practice to emphasize the sparkle of a large diamond or coloured stone by surrounding it with rose-cut diamonds in a setting which neatly followed the outline of the stone. Setting these minute stones called for a precision which made it a difficult and time-consuming process. It was perhaps typical of Fabergé that he revived and perfected this particular art of stone-setting. He was attracted by the elegant effect that the subtle use of rose-diamond bands could achieve.

This is noticeably true of much of his small, decorative jewellery, which includes brooches, pendants, bracelets, necklaces, clasps, cuff links, tiepins and many other items. The tiny stones provide a glitter of diamond sparkle. Precious stones of larger size were mainly cabochon sapphires – very much in demand from the Russian clientèle. As a matter of course Fabergé also used rubies and emeralds.

A stone Fabergé particularly liked was the Mecca stone, which is normally described as a type of cornelian found on the Arabian peninsula. What Fabergé used and called Mecca stone in his stock books was a cabochon chalcedony of a milky light-blue colour not unlike pale sapphires. They also occur in shades of blueish pink, and are sometimes artificially tinted. This stone, which can also be found on a number of *objets d'art*, showed at its best in a surround of rose-cut diamonds. Another typical though much rarer stone was moss agate, a

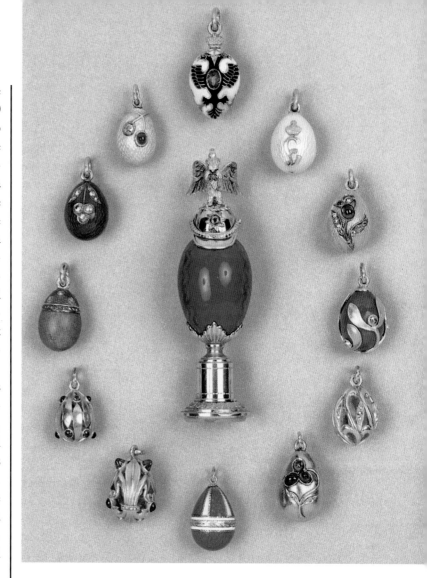

A desk seal with an egg-shaped handle surmounted by the helmet of the Chevalier's Guard Regiment, 6.4 cm (2¼ inches) high, surrounded by a group of miniature Easter eggs by Fabergé and other jewellers

milky white stone with branching, tree-like patterns occurring naturally within it. It was used, for example, as thin oval plaques for brooches.

Enamelwork was a field in which Fabergé excelled, and he used it in decorative jewellery. *Guilloché* enamel in bright red, royal blue, or in more subtle shades of opalescent pink, was used to decorate brooches and pendants. These were made in a great variety of shapes, many of them unique to Fabergé's work shops. More elaborate techniques of enamelling with *paillons* or even with painted miniatures were also used with small jewellery items.

Holmström's Stock Records

A fascinating recent discovery by A. Kenneth Snowman was the stock records of Holmström's workshops. Some of his findings were discussed in the article 'Two Books of Revelation' published in *Apollo* in September 1987. The records are a mine of valuable information about the design, materials, dates and costs of some of the most exquisite works in the field of jewellery.

Every jewel made in Holmström's workshop from 6 March 1909 to 20 March 1915 is recorded with a watercolour drawing, a description of the materials, the quantities of stones with their exact weight, and the cost. According to Ulla Tillander it was Alma Teresia Pihl, August Holmström's granddaughter, who was in charge of making sketches of the workshop's ready-made pieces in 1909 and 1910. The books seem to be a pictorial record of what was produced and what was subsequently transferred to the retail shop, rather than a collection of original designs from which the jeweller had to work.

The great interest and value of these stock books lies in the prodigious quanttity of drawings, which give an idea of the variety of styles, designs and techniques which were used in Fabergé's jewellery workshops.

One example is the jewellery made on the theme of ice or frost crystals. It is thought to have been Alma Teresia Pihl who, after years of making drawings for the stock record books, started designing these original jewels. The story is that a large order for brooches for Emanuel Nobel was placed in late 1911 and had to be executed with great haste. She is said to have been inspired by the ice crystals which formed on draughty office window panes in the cold Russian winter.

A vast quantity of brooches, and later pendants as well, were made to her designs. They featured irregular, star-shaped frost motifs set with rose-cut diamonds in platinum or silver, often mounted on rock crystal simulating ice.

One of the most surprising discoveries in the stock books was a sketch of a circular mosaic brooch made with varicoloured stones, and surrounded by half-pearls and opaque white enamel. The drawing is dated 24 July 1913. The brooch was designed by Alma Pihl, apparently inspired by a piece of petit point embroidery, and seems to have been the prototype for the decoration of the Imperial Mosaic Egg presented by the Tsar to the Empress Alexandra

A page from the stock book of Holmström's workshop showing drawings of jewelled gold and enamelled pendants commemorating the tercentenary of Romanov rule, dated 4 February 1913. The finished pendant is shown next to the drawing

24 Кулона № 1   Кабин. Е.И.В.

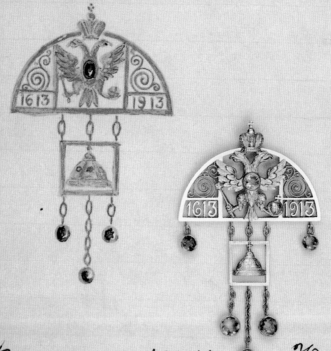

24 Кулона № 11   Кабин. Е.И.В.

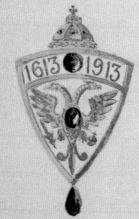

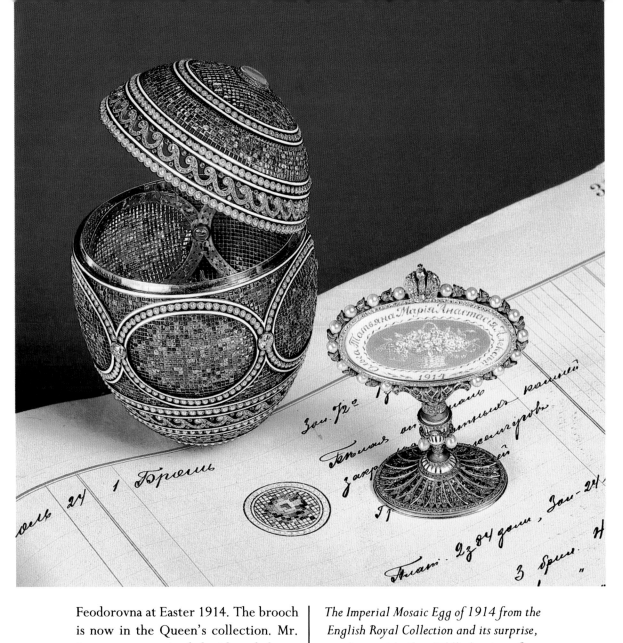

Feodorovna at Easter 1914. The brooch is now in the Queen's collection. Mr. Snowman conceived the idea of photographing the egg and its surprise with the the page of the stock book: the result is illustrated above.

Romanov Tercentenary

In 1913 the workshop's output was apparently concentrated on small pieces of jewellery featuring the state symbols; the double-headed eagles and Monomakh crown, with the dates

The Imperial Mosaic Egg of 1914 from the English Royal Collection and its surprise, shown with Alma Pihl's drawing of 24 July 1913

1613–1913, to mark the Tercentenary of the Romanov rule. They have an openwork design similar to filigree, set with small cabochon sapphires and rubies. The Imperial cabinet had ordered these brooches and pendants as commemorative presents for the Tercentenary celebrations.

Other sketches include brooches of moss agate, Mecca stones, and aquamarines; cuff links and a pendant of carved rhodonite; a more classical brooch in the form of a bow with diamonds and rubies and pendants designed as the crowned initials of the Empresses Marie and Alexandra.

It is fascinating to find sketches dated 1913 showing jewels in a forward-looking style that seems to anticipate the art deco period of the 1920s. They are more geometric and often combine coloured hardstones with diamonds.

Not surprisingly there are hundreds of miniature egg pendants recorded in the stock book. These tiny Easter presents brought Fabergé's firm great fame and success, although they were certainly not his invention. An 18th century jewelled gold pendant in the shape of an egg and containing a jetton with the monogram of Catherine the Great was kept in the treasury of the Winter Palace. It probably served as the prototype for Fabergé's eggs. Other jewellers, especially Friedrich Köchli, also produced small eggs in the last decades of the 19th century. The Köchli eggs are mainly made of gold and set with cabochon stones or diamonds. There were also other jewellers who worked with enamels.

The Fabergé eggs are collectively a *tour de force* of the goldsmith-jewellers art. Many different techniques and materials are used in a great variety of design and decoration. What made these tiny charms so successful is that they were useful as small presents and were pleasing collectables that could be

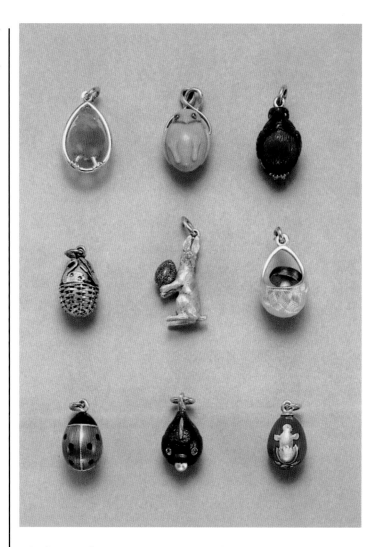

A selection of miniature Easter eggs and, in the centre, a pendant of an Easter bunny holding an aventurine egg. In the top row are hardstone birds in gold mounts by Fedor Afanassiev and Henrik Wigström. The mushroom in the egg-shaped basket is marked with the initials KΦ. (Forbes Collection)

worn on chains and necklaces.

George, the son of The Duke of Mecklenburg-Strelitz gives a typical

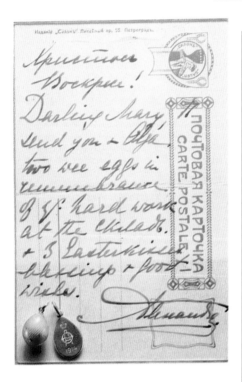

Easter card written by Empress Alexandra,
a green enamel miniature egg decorated
with gold stars by Fedor Afanassiev and an
egg-shaped gold charm bearing the
Empress's monogram and the date 1914.
(Forbes Collection)

picture of how the miniature Easter eggs were worn in Russia in his description of Easter 1916 at the palace of grand Duchess Vladimir, Marie of Mecklenburg-Schwerin:

Mama and my sisters were wearing very elegant light-coloured dresses and had one or more necklaces with small eggs made of precious stones. These eggs were made by the jewellers of St Petersburg from widely differing types of stone. They were the size of a cherry or a grape and were suspended by small gold links

from a chain. It was a custom at Easter to give them as presents not only to members of the family but also to distant cousins and old friends. My sisters each had two or three long chains studded with these eggs which hung down to their waists.

That enthusiasm for miniature Easter eggs was not confined to the Russian clientèle can be seen from the sales ledgers of Fabergé's London branch. In the spring of 1912, just before Easter, 30 eggs were sold within ten days, the majority of them decorated with vari-coloured enamel. King George V and Queen Mary acquired an "Egg, elephant, nephrite, gold ring, 2 roses" for £3.15s on 28 March. Other eggs included one in light green and white opalescent enamel (£1.4s); one of amethyst and diamonds (£4); a steel grey enamel (13s); one in the shape of a seal in nephrite and red enamel (£5); and one described as "Egg, Kingfisher, agate, £5". The list from the sales ledgers dating from 1907 to 1917 also includes eggs of surprising design such as a red jasper squirrel, a lapis lazuli dove, one with Mecca stone roses and red enamel, a grey jasper owl and even an orletz pig which was bought by Grand Duke Kyrill in April 1913 for £8.

Commemorative Eggs
Enamel and hardstone eggs, some of them jewelled, with decorations inspired by flowers and animals, probably form the largest group. But there are also quite a number of egg-shaped pen-

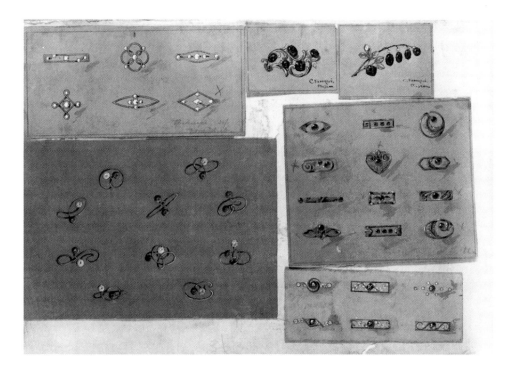

A group of original working drawings for jewelled brooches from Fabergé's Moscow branch

dants whose decoration has a commemorative character, based, for example, on the year of presentation. Some eggs are surmounted by helmets of the Imperial guard regiments; emblems of orders such as the Cross of St. George, crowned ciphers of members of the Imperial family, and double-headed eagles, are other themes. From the beginning of the war in 1914 the Red Cross emblem became increasingly popular on eggs which were sold at charity events.

Most Fabergé eggs can be distinguished from eggs made by other jewellers by their generous size and bold decoration. Nearly all of them are gold mounted and were marked on the suspension ring rather than on the smaller ring fixed to the egg. Workmasters who have been recorded as makers of miniature Easter eggs are Erik Kollin,

Michael Perchin, Henrik Wigström, August Hollming, August and Albert Holmström, Fedor Afanassiev and Oskar Pihl. The initials of other workmasters also occur. A large number of eggs show the mark with the Cyrillic initials КФ in an oval as the signature of the firm. Due to lack of space the mark with the full name of Fabergé was never applied.

Unfortunately the suspension rings bearing the marks very often broke and were lost, especially when they were removed from long necklaces by inexperienced jewellers. As a result many eggs can now be attributed to Fabergé only on stylistic or technical grounds and by comparison with other signed ones.

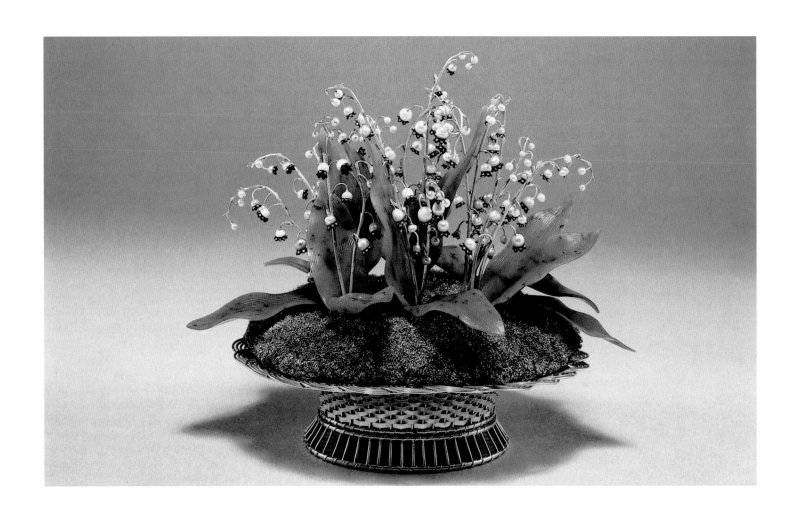

*The basket of lilies-of-the-valley by August
Holmström which was presented to the
Empress Alexandra Feodorovna in 1896.
It stood on her desk until the Revolution in
1917. (M. G. Gray Foundation Collection,
New Orleans)*

Chapter Four

FLOWER STUDIES

Nine lilies-of-the-valley, their leaves made of nephrite and their flowers made of pearls tipped with rose-cut diamonds, grow on gold stems in golden moss set in a golden wickerwork basket. It is Fabergé's earliest-known flower study, and stood for many years on the desk of the Tsarina Alexandra. Flower studies are amongst the most beautiful, the most delicate, and the rarest of Fabergé's creations. Yet the variety of flowers produced is striking – each one a test and demonstration of the imagination, ingenuity and artistry of its creator. The charm and naturalism of the Fabergé flower studies are a triumph of both craft and design.

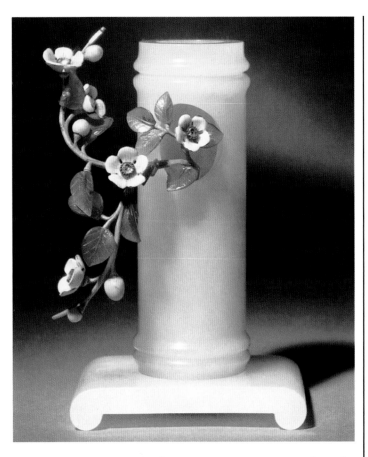

most extravagant display seems to have been the one at the apartment of Countess Mordvinoff around 1914. She had her marble bathroom fitted with crystal glass shelves where the jewelled flower studies would sparkle in the perfumed steam of the bath.

Japanese Inspiration

Fabergé's flower studies count among his most elegant and beautiful creations. They are striking because of their simplicity: single stems, with only a few flower-heads in bright enamel colours contrasting with dark green nephrite leaves. The most likely source of inspiration seems to be the Japanese art of flower arranging, ikebana. Not surprisingly there are a number of Japanese-style flower studies mentioned in the London sales ledgers, especially around 1907 and 1908. They include a Japanese lotus, Japanese pine, and a cherry. Japanese art was, however, also a source of the art nouveau movement, which was itself much concerned with floral themes.

Historical sources for the design of Fabergé's flowers are often suggested. Jewelled flower bouquets, for instance, studded with foiled diamonds and coloured semiprecious stones, were made in the 18th century. There are

After Easter supper Grand Duchess Vladimir distributed fabulous presents. She herself received beautiful things, for instance small flowerpots made from hardstone with imitations of flowers on stems of precious materials, all fantastic jeweller's work.

This appears in an account of the court Easter festivities in 1916, written by George, the son of the Duke of Mecklenburg-Strelitz. Flower studies were in fact, apart from miniature egg-pendants, the favourite choice of Easter gift for a lady. They were then usually displayed on tables or in cabinets. The

Above: *Japonica spray with enamelled flowers and nephrite leaves in a bowenite 'Bamboo' vase on a white quartz pedestal*
Opposite: *From the left, catkins of spun green gold, mock orange of white quartz and bleeding heart with flowers of rhodonite (English Royal Collection)*

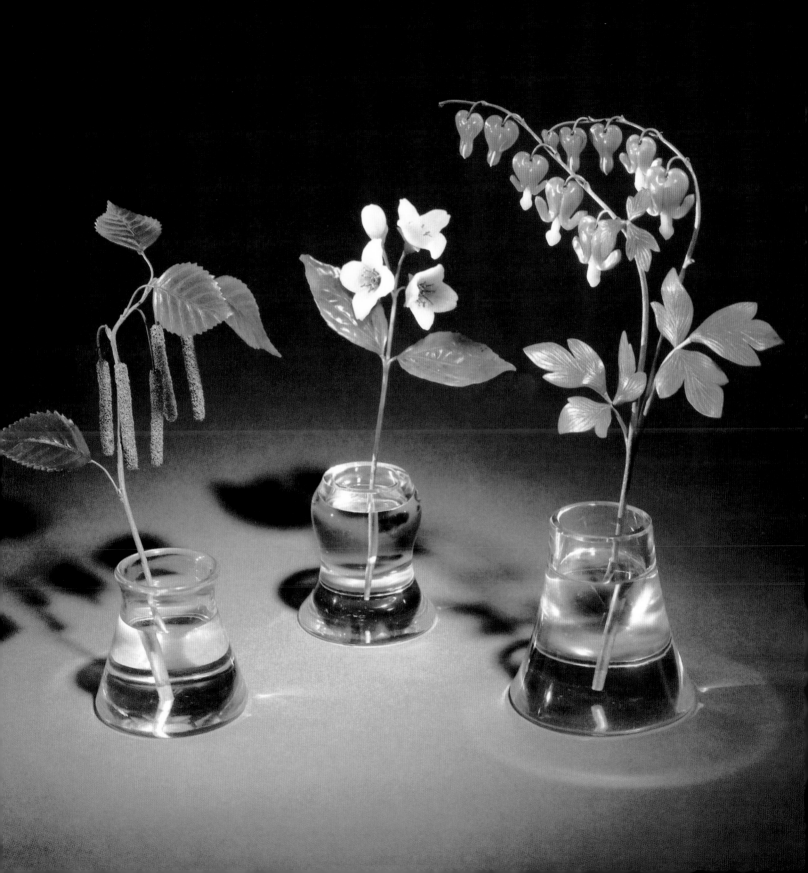

three such flower arrangements, which must have been known to Fabergé, in the Hermitage treasury. One of them is a lily set with diamonds and pearls which stands in a rock-crystal vase. In the mid-19th century at the 1851 Great Exhibition in London 'Haulick's Jewel Flower' attracted special attention and it was illustrated and described in the catalogue. The flower, a carnation in full bloom, was set with diamonds and rubies. It had a gold stem and leaves of emerald green enamel and stood in a gold vase. Made by the jeweller Friedrich G. Haulick of Hanau, near Frankfurt, it foreshadows Fabergé's creations in so far as it is highly naturalistic, with one flowerhead, a large bud and curling leaves.

Lifelike Flowers

Fabergé's flowers are very realistic and he used every means at his disposal to make his flowers imitate nature. A buttercup with flowers of gold and yellow enamel looks as light as the real thing. The stem stands in a vase of flawless rock crystal which appears to contain water. This *trompe-l'oeil* technique of carving the crystal makes the naturalistic effect even more striking. Then look at the details: the petals are finely engraved under translucent yellow enamel to simulate the veins, the golden stems are engraved with microscopically thin lines. There are other flower studies where undulating nephrite leaves seem to grow from the stem, which in some cases is also enamelled.

The naturalism of Fabergé flowers, however, has an artistic side. They are

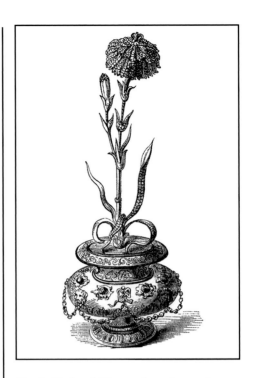

Haulick's Jewel Flower, from the catalogue of the Great Exhibition, 1851

more than just a 'photographic rendering of nature', as some critics said of Fabergé's exhibits at the Paris *Exposition Universelle* of 1900. They present an interpretation of nature.

In some cases different plants share the same single stem – a cornflower with oats or with buttercups, for example. Even the changes of the seasons seem to have been ignored when a sprig of wild cherry is shown bearing both flower and fruit. Fabergé used these artistic devices to enhance the naturalistic effect.

Opposite: *Mistletoe with nephrite leaves and moonstone berries in a rock crystal vase, 13.3 cm (5½ inches) high*

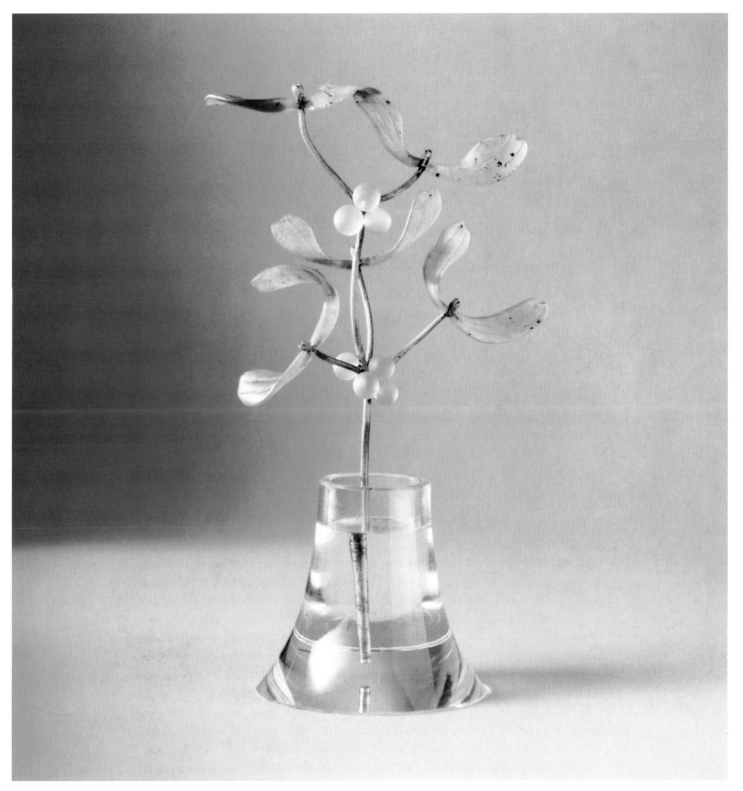

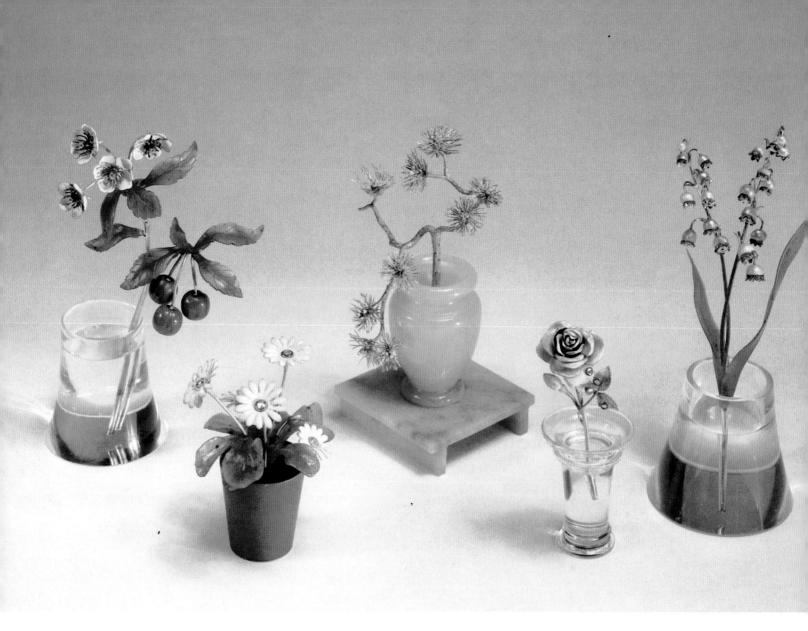

*A group of flower studies from the English
Royal Collection. The gold pine tree cost
£52 on 14 December 1908*

The most popular flower in Russia
around the turn of the century was the
lily-of-the-valley – the favourite flower
of the Empress Alexandra. At her
coronation in 1896 she received a jewelled basket of lilies-of-the-valley from
the merchant guild of Nizhny Nov-
gorod. This is the earliest of Fabergé
flower arrangements and, according to
the Russian *Town and Country* magazine
of 1914, it used to stand on her desk.
Nine lily-of-the-valley plants are em-
bedded in a mossy cushion of spun gold.
The flower sprays have chased gold
stems, nephrite leaves and pearl flowers
tipped with rose-cut diamonds. The
yellow gold basket imitates wickerwork and the diamond-set pearl flower

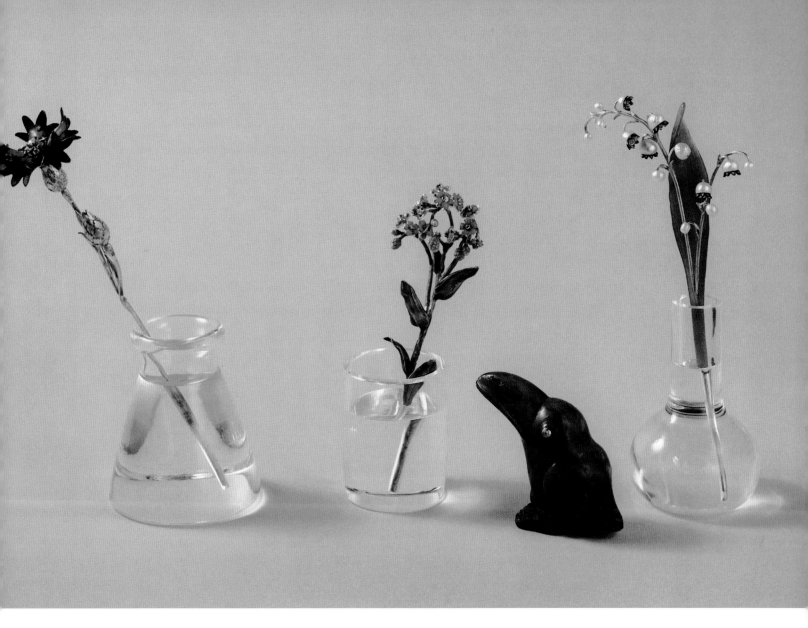

heads give a sparkling effect to the whole composition. Their setting so obviously involved a skilled jeweller's hand that it comes as no surprise to discover that the basket is signed by Fabergé's chief jeweller August Holmström.

Among the recently discovered stock records of jewellery by Holmström there is another flower design exquisitely painted in watercolour. It shows a spray of forget-me-nots with turquoise petals and diamond centres, placed in a rock crystal vase. This watercolour is dated 12 May 1912. A. Kenneth Snowman describes it in detail in his splendid article 'Two Books of Revelations':

1912.

Май 12 Кольцо Platine.

1 саф. д. 139. } саг.
12 брил. 229. }
дв. 20 ноис. 10. рід
36 роз: 24 розмѣ 8
12 " 12

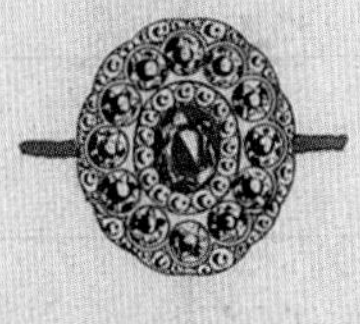

" Цвѣтокъ „незабудка"

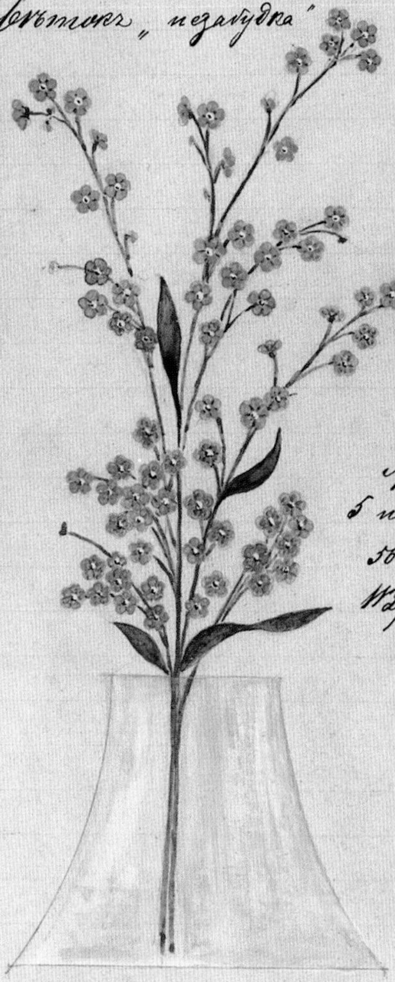

Хрусталь - ед
5 нефрит. листр. ед
565 бирюза
№ роз:
46 розмѣ 8
25 " 9
36 " 10
6 " 12

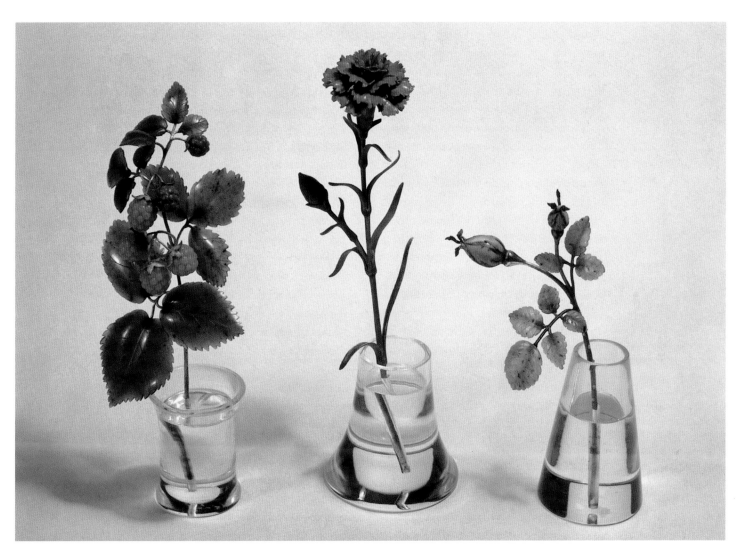

The very fact that a flower design should figure among those for jewels seems to demonstrate that, although the stems of these studies are sometimes physically stamped with the marks of the goldsmith, their nature is, in a sense, ambiguous, growing in some sort of no man's land or neutral soil between *objet de vitrine* and jewel.

Holmström's jewellery workshop must have been involved in the production of those flowers which are most elaborately decorated with precious

Opposite: *A page from Holmström's stock book showing a forget-me-not and details of the stones needed to make it up*

Above: *Raspberries carved from rhodonite and jade, an enamelled carnation and rosebuds with leaves of nephrite. (English Royal Collection)*

stones. Most of the flower studies, however, are not signed or even hall-marked because of lack of space on the delicate gold stems, which would in any case have been disfigured by a punch.

There are on the other hand some flowers, admittedly rare, which are signed by Fabergé's head workmaster Henrik Wigström. Of 20 flower studies in the Royal collections, for example, only two have Wigström's mark. Even more rare is the full Fabergé signature, though it appears on the rowanberry sprig from Miss Yznaga's collection. According to Bäcksbacka, an authority on Russian goldsmiths, one workmaster who did not have the right to sign his works was P. M. Kremlev. He was responsible for the hardstone polishing and the assembling of the leaves, fruit, berries and composite vases.

Although the rock crystal vases with simulated water made Fabergé's flower studies both popular and famous there are a number of flower studies in vases made of opaque hardstones such as agate, bowenite, jasper, or lapis lazuli. One such piece appears in the London sales ledgers: 'Plant – Japanese lotus. Flower white opalescent enamel & roses, branches gold, leaves nephrite, vase brown orletz and rock crystal.' It was sold on 16 March 1908 for £35 to Mrs Sackville West.

The sales ledgers also show how rare flower studies are in Fabergé's *oeuvre*. In the period from 1907 to 1917 nearly 10,000 items were sold in London: only 35 flower studies are mentioned. The complete list of these flower studies, in spite of the occasionally whimsical spelling and phraseology characteristic of the London sales ledgers, gives an idea of the diversity of the flowers produced. It is, however, remarkable that there are no lilies-of-the-valley.

Burberry	Raspberry Bush
Branch of Roses	Cornflower & Oats
Marguerite Daisy	Birch Branch
Cherry	Rose Tree Pruner
Blackberries	Red Currants
Japanese Flower	Whortleberry
Convolvulus	Jasmine
Japanese Lotus	Daffodil
Vase of Violets	Bluebells
Pensée	Crocus
Chrysanthemum	Pansy
Crategus Branch	Nasturtium
Holly	Cactus
Japanese Pine	Mistletoe Sprig
Japanese Cherry	Jessamine
Japanese Flower	Sweet Pea
in Bamboo	Narcissus
Snowdrop	Forget-me-not

The chrysanthemum, the most expensive flower, and was sold for £117 to Mrs S. Poklewski on 27 November 1908. It is not decorated with diamonds or other precious stones: its value lies in the fine, delicate enamelling of the thin petals in opaque pink and yellow. It stands in a square rock crystal vase and is signed by Henrik Wigström. Today it is in the English Royal Collection.

As most of the flowers are unsigned the question that naturally frequently arises is: how can a piece confidently be attributed to Fabergé? This is especially difficult because Fabergé's ideas in this area were copied by his contempor-

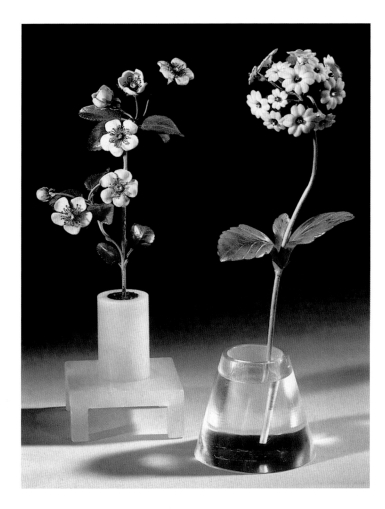

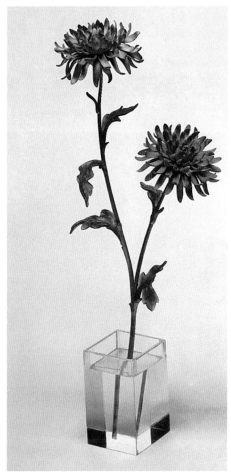

Left: A spray of gentians in the Japanese style and a honey flower with an opaque enamel bloom in a rock crystal vase

Right: Enamelled chrysanthemum by Henrik Wigström.

aries. Later in the 1920s his sons had flower studies made in Paris, where Cartier was also producing similar work, though more in the art déco style. The hardstone workshops of Idar Oberstein were also active, and apparently specialized in making raspberry stems in rock crystal vases.

In trying to decide whether a flower is an original or a fake there are a few main points to look at. Fabergé's flowers are delicately made and show minute naturalistic details, such as chased, rounded, stems finely engraved to imitate natural variations. The stems were made exclusively of gold, never silver, and they stand at an angle or lean on the edge of the vase, whereas copies stand rigidly upright without any support. Even different plants are brought together on a single stem: separately visible stems in a crystal vase seem to be a sure sign of a fake.

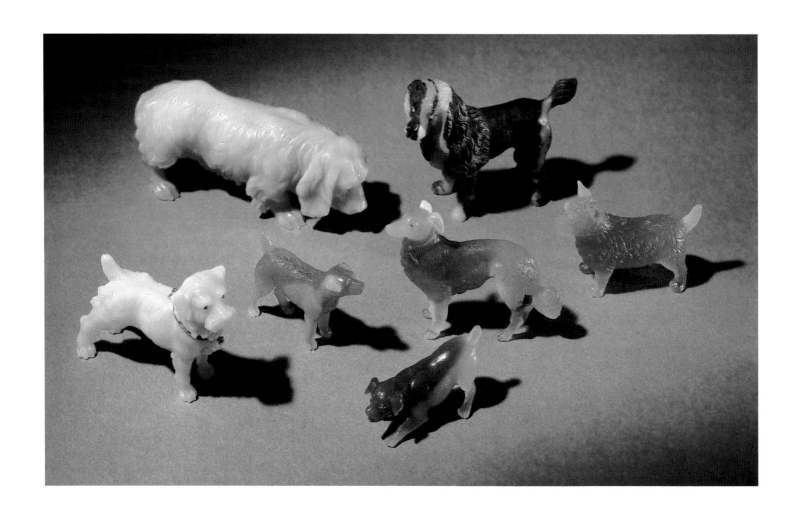

*A group of hardstone dogs from the English
Royal Collection. On the left is Caesar,
King Edward VII's Norfolk terrier, carved
in white chalcedony with cabochon ruby eyes
and an enamelled collar inscribed
'I belong to the King'*

Chapter Five

HARDSTONE CARVINGS

As an artist-jeweller Fabergé was fascinated by the colour, beauty, pattern and texture of Russian hardstones. Inspired largely by Japanese examples, and especially by netsuke, of which he had a significant collection, he created hardstone figures of animals that found enthusiastic buyers and admirers, including royal patrons, both within and beyond the boundaries of Europe. Many of these carvings had features – eyes, legs, beaks, and claws – enhanced by jeweller's skills with gems and precious metals. Some of his finest hardstone carvings are figurines, sometimes almost caricatures, of characters from history, literature, and everyday life in Russia, assembled by the *commesso* technique from a variety of contrasting hardstones.

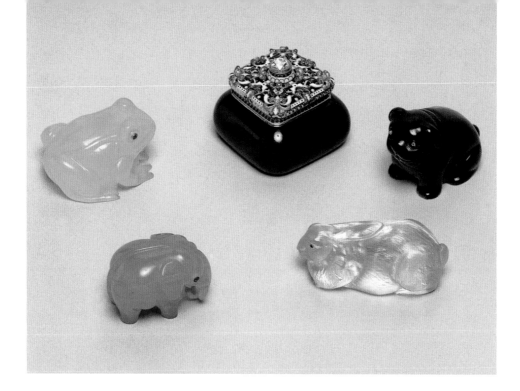

Fabergé was fascinated by the beauty and colour of Russian hardstones and he brought the art of cutting and polishing them to perfection. In this he was once again turning to a craft already well established in Russia, but adding elaborate new technical methods and styles to create objects of the highest artistic quality.

Lapidaries had existed in Russia since the 18th century, the most famous being those at Ekaterinburg in the Urals and the Peterhof stone-polishing factory near St Petersburg. They were known for their massive vases, furniture and decorative objects made of malachite, Kalgan jasper, agate and other stones. Around 1850 paperweights and desk ornaments in the form of models of fruit and flowers were made from composite, carved semiprecious stones: but with mass production they were becoming increasingly clumsy and less detailed. In order to achieve the highest possible standards, Fabergé decided to open a stone-cutting workshop of his own, which he had bought from Karl Woerffel.

Fabergé's workmaster for hardstones was the artist P. M. Kremlev. With a large staff including artists and craftsmen, he specialized in producing small hardstone models: animals, figurines, flower studies and many other types of objects ranging from parasol handles to pillboxes.

To meet the demand for these hardstone objects, which were greatly admired by western European clients, Fabergé would also buy in pieces already carved, some of them from established workshops. They would then receive their finishing touches and final polish in his own workshops. A nephrite box, manufactured at Peterhof and encrusted in gold with a landscape view in the Japanese taste, is an example of this cooperation.

Animal Models

It is with hardstone animal sculptures that Fabergé may be said to have brought this aspect of his art to a peak of achievement. His production of animal models started in about 1900.

Fabergé attached great importance to both the technical quality of the carving and the aesthetic quality of the style. Although these small models have been described as 'realistic', this impression is not always due to a painstakingly detailed reproduction of external appearances. Most of them in fact observe exactly that distortion of the full-scale proportions that successful miniaturization requires. Their 'realism' usually lies in an inspired choice of material coupled with a sympathetic choice of posture – a posture which, by the angle of the head or the positioning of the paws or tail, somehow conveys the very essence of the animal.

This quality in the Fabergé objects may be related to the interest in Japanese art which developed in Europe from about 1880 onwards. This applies to the flowers as well as to the animals, which are similar to netsuke figures. It is known that Carl Fabergé owned a collection of netsuke, which after 1918, was acquired by the Hermitage, Leningrad.

Apart from the fashionable interest in Japanese art, Fabergé profited from

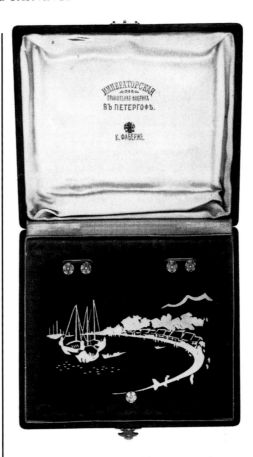

A nephrite box with gold mounts in the Japanese style, in its original case

the special affection that the English Royal family had for the animals of their country estate at Sandringham. King Edward VII, moreover, was a devoted racegoer. One of Fabergé's most important commissions was to make models of Queen Alexandra's favourite animals (Queen Alexandra was a sister of the Russian Empress Maria Feodorovna). The commission included not only her dogs, but an entire farm with cows, bulls, chickens, cockerels, turkeys and ducks. The horses included the King's Derby winner, Persimmon.

As early as 1906 Fabergé had set up a

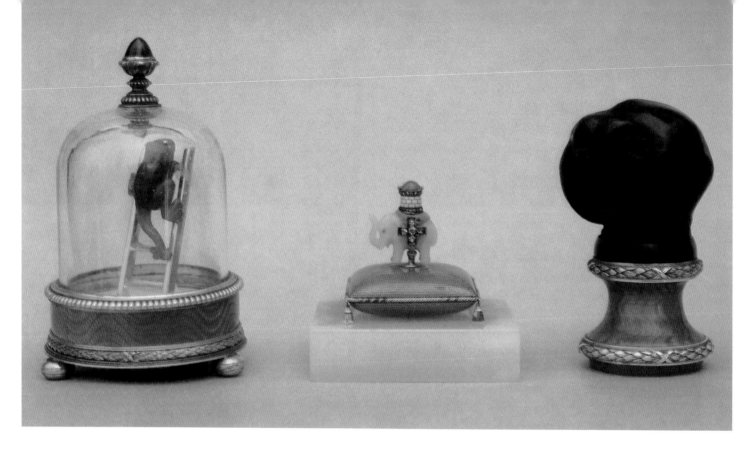

London branch at 48 Dover Street in order to meet the demand for objects from the Royal family. Although the main shop in St Petersburg was far more important, the London branch is of special interest today because its sales records have been preserved. These contain information about the customers, and the number and prices of objects sold.

One example is from the financial year running from 14 July 1910 to 13 July 1911; during this period 26 animal figures were sold. The most expensive was a grey jade owl with gold legs and diamond eyes, which was bought by Mr. Gordon Bennett on 3 January 1911 for £65.15s. The cheapest was an agate turtle purchased by the Baronne Albert de Goldschmidt on 14 June 1911 for £6.10s. On 26 November 1910 the model of a Yorkshire terrier named Caesar is recorded in the ledgers. The collar carries the inscription 'I belong to the King': Caesar was King Edward VII's favourite dog, and the carving was bought by the Hon. Mrs. R. Greville for £35 as a memento of the King, who had died in May of that year.

Each year between 1907 and 1917 an average sale of 25 animal figures is recorded: altogether, Fabergé sold about 250 animals in London, but the number sold in Russia must have been much larger.

The best known artist-modellers were Boris Froedman-Cluzel, Eugenia Petrovna Ilinskaya-Andreoletti and Elena Shishkina, all of whom specialized in animals. There were also quite a number of artists working in the St Petersburg workshop whose names have not been recorded. Most of them worked by copying originals or by using stuffed animals as models or by making copies from Fabergé's netsuke collection.

The animal figures fall into three groups. First, there is a considerable number of animals with gold, silver-gilt, or, less frequently, silver mounts. There is no doubt that these are by Fabergé: the mounts had to be stamped, and were also in many cases signed, and often carry the mark of the work-master. Among them are functional as well as decorative objects: handles for walking-sticks, umbrellas and seals; bell-pushes, boxes, and even bird-cages. The miniature Easter eggs are a special case: measuring no more than 2 cm ($\frac{3}{4}$ inch), these are tiny animals carved as egg-shaped pendants. There are quartz chickens with gold mounts made by Fedor Afanassiev, and the Forbes Collection boasts a jade kingfisher. On 14 March 1908 the London records mention the sale of an 'Egg, Owl, Gold Legs, garnet Eyes' for £4.15s. To Mr. Waldorf Astor'.

In the second group come animal figures with small gold mounts – mostly the legs or beaks of birds. When the size permitted the metal parts were signed and stamped. These were made almost exclusively by Henrik Wigström, the

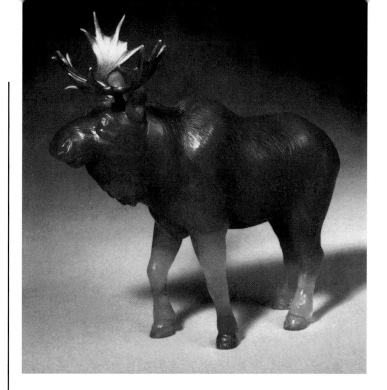

A moose carved from brown agate with gold antlers and diamond eyes.
11 cm (4$\frac{1}{2}$ inches) long

chief workmaster between 1903 and 1918 or, in a few instances, by his predecessor Michael Perchin.

The animal sculptures made solely of semiprecious stones form the last and probably the most important group. Identifying the artists is most difficult for they are usually unsigned. These pieces are distinguished by a technical precision of stone-cutting aimed at achieving a realistic finish. It is best seen in the chasing on the hide or plumage of the animals or birds. Only under a magnifying glass can one detect the thousands of lines that represent the fur on a miniature mouse only 3 cm (1$\frac{1}{4}$ inches) in length. The heavily polished nephrite frogs and toads have an almost wet gloss, and their legs and claws are individually sculpted and refined to the tiniest detail. There are never any sharp edges: the finished surface of these animal models at their best seems like a wax-like, softened substance, rounded on all sides.

The selection of the stone before it was carved was of great importance. A striped or dotted agate, for example, is used for a tiger's or a dog's coat. An agate is chosen for a chimpanzee, so that the pale hands and face match the brown skin. With such choices the artist demonstrates his skill: in order to produce these effects he must first make a study of the multi-layered stones.

Less frequently the realistically carved animals are put together from more than one kind of stone. In the English Royal Collection there is a magpie made of white quartz and a gleaming blue-black labradorite, and an obsidian cockerel with a shiny red purpurine comb.

Animal eyes are usually rose-cut diamonds or green olivines glued into pierced cavities, but larger animals have ruby or sapphire cabochons or, more rarely, brilliant-cut diamonds in gold mounts, sometimes foiled with yellow enamel.

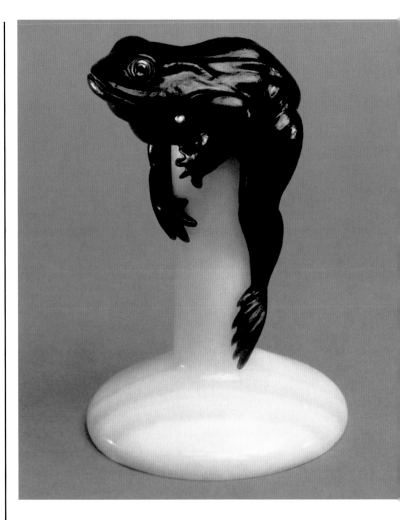

A frog with diamond eyes, realistically carved from nephrite, climbing an onyx base

Animal Caricatures

A special category of stone carvings consists of stylized or caricaturized animals combined with elaborate treatment of detail. Here the influence of Japanese netsuke is at its most obvious. These button-like accessories were used to tie the *sagemono* purse to the sash of the traditional kimono. Made of wood, ivory, horn, amber and semi-precious stones, they frequently represent animals of an even, rounded shape. However, the masters of netsuke were striving to emphasize the grotesque rather than the naturalistic in the movement or position of the animal. In order to do that they studied live animals very carefully, and the result was often what could be called a psychological study of animal behaviour. Fabergé, himself a great collector of netsuke, adapted this form of representation for a large number of his animals, including monkeys, mice and sparrows. Like netsuke these figures need to be touched and held in the hand. As Geoffrey Munn has pointed out in his article 'Fabergé and Japan' in *The Antique Collector*, the artists in St Petersburg also used the *ittobori* style. This is a more geometric interpretation of the shape of an animal. Kingfishers were carved in this style, some of which can be found in the Royal collections. Apart from parallels with netsuke some of Fabergé's animals suggest a stylistic influence derived from Japanese bronzes. In this category there are figures of turkeys, coiled snakes and crabs.

Exaggeration

In his animal caricatures form and expression are exaggerated. Elephants and hippopotamuses of nephrite, chalcedony and bowenite, with wrinkled skin and clumsy bodies, are perhaps the best known. Figures entitled in the sales ledgers 'Pig Smiling' (of satuarn, £14 on 20 November, 1913, to Queen Alexandra) or 'Comic Bird' (of jade, £13.10s. on 30 October 1908, to Lord Alington), almost seem like prototypes of Walt Disney characters.

All sorts of hardstones were used for the figures – agate, jade, nephrite, bowenite, even petrified (fossilised) wood. The only 'stone' which has enabled accurate attribution is purpurine, an artificial material produced of fused glass. Around 1900 it was used exclusively in the Fabergé workshop.

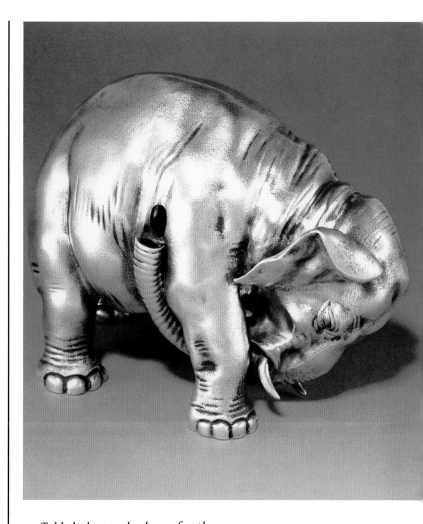

Table lighter in the shape of a silver elephant, the trunk holds the wick. 10.7 cm ($4\frac{1}{4}$ inches) long

A final problem in identifying a Fabergé piece with certainty is caused by duplicates of animal figures. Fabergé made it a point never to produce any of his objects in multiple editions. However, many similar animals frequently recur, obviously because of great demand from his customers. His elephants, for example, which were very popular around 1900, exist in large

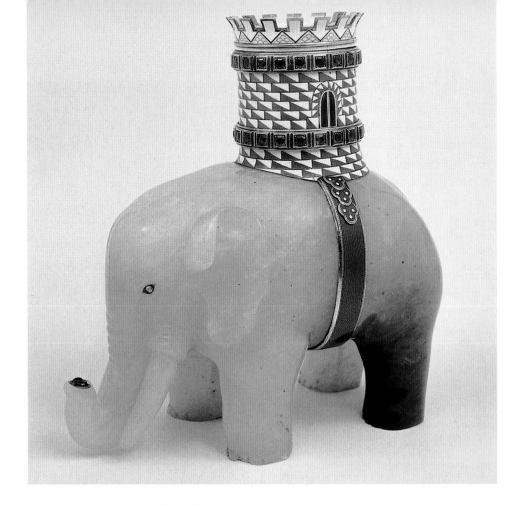

numbers. Often the sole difference is
the variety of stone, which can sometimes only be identified under a magnifying glass. With the sea lions and
kiwi figures, the different versions can
occasionally be distinguished, after
close examination, by the slightly different position of the heads and legs.
Such figures, evidently modelled on the
same originals, differ only in minor
details. For these reasons identification
often depends upon the authenticity of
the fitted cases, which were usually
made of light maple with silk and velvet
linings. The inside of the box shows the
double-headed eagle with the mark of
Fabergé below it. While the silver and
gold objects almost always have their
inventory numbers scratched on, the
hardstone figures do not. On the
wooden cases the number, inscribed by
hand, was only rarely added.

For the collector today the provenance of a piece is increasingly important, and catalogues of exhibitions and
of auctions of historical collections have
a significant role to play.

Queen Elizabeth II owns the most
comprehensive collection of Fabergé
animal figures which is based on Queen
Alexandra's collection. It consists of
about 170 pieces and is a major source

for comparisons. Royal collections, however, rarely appear on the art market, but in 1957 the collection of the King of the Hellenes was auctioned, and in 1981 the collection belonging to the Grand Duchess Marie Alexandrovna, Duchess of Edinburgh, was sold in Geneva.

Provenance

Exhibition catalogues are valuable sources for indications of provenance. For example, at the Russian Art Exhibition in London in 1935, three animal collections were put on display. They belonged to Lady Juliet Duff, Mademoiselle Yznaga (sister of the Duchess of Manchester), and Lady Zia Wernher, who was the daughter of the Grand Duke Michael Michailovitch. The catalogue lists a total of 80 figures.

Animal figures in the style of Fabergé, and sometimes straight copies, had already started to appear by 1900.

Sumin and Denisov-Uralsky were working in St Petersburg, like Fabergé. In Paris Cartier sold animals in the Russian style, produced there by Varangoz-Lavabre, Fréville and Césard at the Taillerie de Royat, or made in Russia by Ovchinnikov and Denisov. At the hardstone workshops in Idar-Oberstein Fabergé animals served as standard models.

Forgeries, as in most art fields, may be detected only through an intensive study of the genuine article. This applies first and foremost to the hall marks and signatures (the Fabergé mark) on gold or silver. In so far as they refer to specific workmasters and craftsmen, these marks follow a certain system. The gold parts of animal figures normally carry the Fabergé mark together with the initials of Henrik Wigström, or in rarer cases those of Michael Perchin. Other mounts, and especially those with enamels, are likely to be signed by the workmaster who did the enamelling. Craftsmen who worked in silver, like Julius Rappoport, never produced animals of semiprecious stone. Hardstone animals were produced exclusively in the St Petersburg workshop.

Grey jade parrot with a purpurine tail in a silver cage: a carving, from life, of the Empress Marie Feodorovna's favourite parrot. 16.5 cm (6½ inches) high

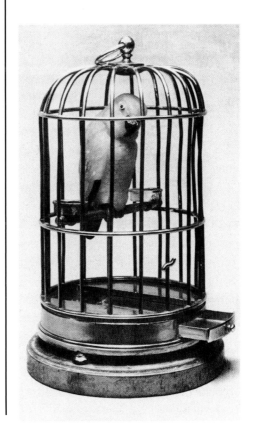

FIGURINES

Figurines assembled from various different kinds of semiprecious stones are the most unusual and controversial items produced by the Fabergé workshops. Together with the Imperial Easter eggs they are among the rarest objects Fabergé produced. Bainbridge thought that no more than 50 were made: but since 47 have been traced to date, the total production may have amounted to between 60 and 80 figures altogether.

Usually depicting genre figures, these stone sculptures are all characterized by a high degree of realism. This and the folkloric aspect of these small figurines – they stand between 10 and 20 cm (4 and 8 inches) in height – have led to much dispute about their artistic artistic value. Some critics consider them the worst possible kitsch, comparable to garden gnomes. In pre-revolutionary Russia they did service as table decorations, a style that has since gone out of fashion.

As far as artistic sources are concerned, parallels can be found between the Fabergé figurines and the Russian porcelain figures and groups made during the second half of the 19th century. This is particularly true of the porcelain work produced by the Gardner factory in Moscow. From 1860 onwards the Gardner and Kuznetsov factories produced painted biscuitware figures which were to become extremely popular in Russia until the turn of the century.

Opposite: *Four composite hardstone figurines of Russian genre types, about 13.3 cm (5½ inches) high. The man carrying a water pitcher on his head has the signature FABERGÉ engraved under his left boot and the inventory number 25748 under the right*

Below: *Porcelain figure by the Gardner Factory, Moscow, circa 1870*

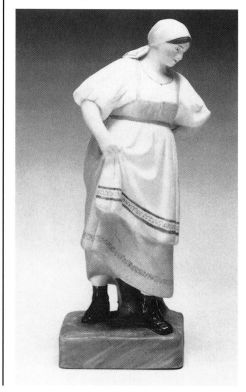

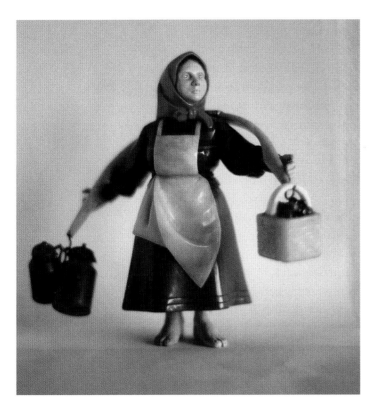
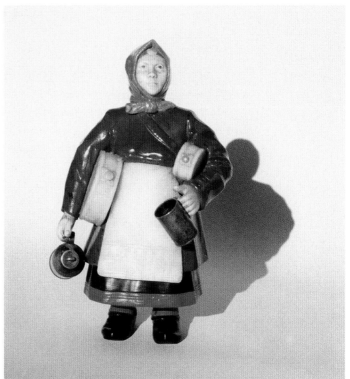
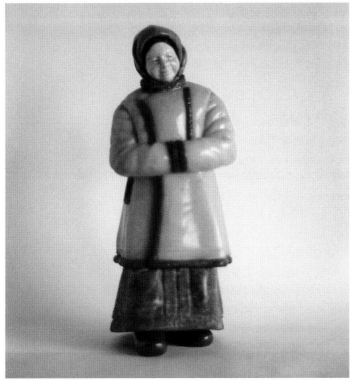
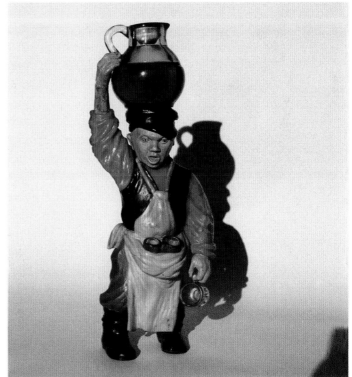

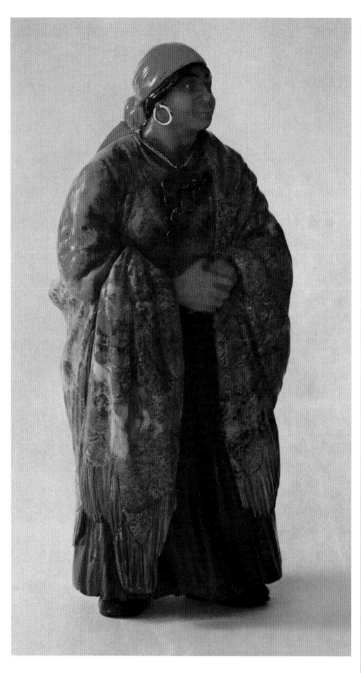

Portrait sculpture of the gipsy singer, Varya Panina, carved in hardstone. 17.8 cm (7 inches) high

Porcelain figures produced in the first half of the 19th century were narrative and humorous in character, based on figures taken from contemporary literature and from the popular *lubok* picture stories. After about 1860 they tended to become more realistic, probably as a result of the work of the *Peredwizhniki* or Travelling Art Exhibition Association. This movement preached a realistic and socially critical approach to painting, an idea which found expression in the work of Repin, Wasnetsov and Makovski, who were mainly concerned with portraying the life of the Russian people. This subject matter was taken up and expressed in the porcelain figures. Typical Gardner factory products are, for example figures of a building worker wielding a spade and a drunken peasant performing a dance. This interest in realistic representation is apparent in the detail of the costumes, the movements of the figures, and the overall impression they make.

Concierge Figures

These biscuit porcelain groups, which were known as 'concierge figures' since they were frequently to be seen in porters' lodges, were in mass production by 1900 and had become widely popular. Fabergé was able to make them acceptable to more exclusive circles by making them from precious materials. He added the occasional element of caricature to his versions too, 'petrifying' the dancing peasant in his exaggerated movements and capturing the stiffness of the soldier standing to attention. This element of caricature is also to be found in the detailed portrayals of the marriage-broker and a painter.

Fabergé's use of semiprecious stones for these figures harks back to the 17th century Florentine art of hardstone carving. A striking example of this influence can be seen in the Museo degli Argenti in Florence. It is a group of six apostles, an evangelist and an archangel; these figures, which are about 35.5 cm (14 inches) high, were designed by Giovanni Bilivert sometime after 1605 for the ciborium in the Chapel of San Lorenzo in Florence. They were modelled in wax by the sculptor Orazio Mochi and carved in semiprecious stones by Milanese hardstone cutters using the *commesso* technique. The attitudes and postures of these figures as well as the choice of vivid colours for the stones are typical of the later period of mannerism.

It was an obvious step for Fabergé to start producing similar stone *commesso* work, especially since semiprecious stones from the Urals and Siberia were already being extensively used in the production of his *objets d'art*.

In contrast to figures carved from only one kind of stone (one of these is a caricature of Queen Victoria commissioned by Grand Duke Nicholas Nicholaievich), those made from more than one kind of stone date from after the turn of the century. The first one sold in London was recorded in 1908, while others are engraved 1913 and 1915. Assay marks stamped on the silver or gold parts date the figures to the period between 1908 and 1917.

The figures can be classified into three groups: folkloric genre figures, portrait sculptures, and figures modelled on characters from history and literature. The folkloric category is the most extensive one and includes figures of peasants and their wives, craftsmen, street vendors, coachmen, tradesmen, policemen and soldiers. Each individual character is imbued with remarkable liveliness, both in posture and facial expression. The peasant boy sitting on a wooden bench and singing to his balalaika can be regarded as the epitome of Russian country life.

Portrait Sculptures

In some figures realism led to a portrait-like quality, as in the case of the *dvornik* or houseboy who worked at Fabergé's premises in St Petersburg and who is wearing peaked cap bearing the address *24 Morskaya*. Although the move to portrait sculpture seemed a logical one, very few such figures were ever made. The best known one is of Varya Panina, a gypsy who sang in ohe village of Yar, near Moscow renowned among officers of the Guard for its boisterous parties. Varya Panina, who became a star attraction because of her superb voice, was the focus of a tragic scandal: she died on stage singing 'My heart is breaking . . .' after having taken poison because of an unhappy love affair. Fabergé's stone sculpture of her, measuring an unusually tall 16 cm (6½ inches), shows her in a green jasper dress, with a shawl of red and white jasper and a purpurine headsquare.

Another celebrated portrait figure is that of Pustinikov, the bodyguard of the Empress Maria Feodorovna, who from 1894 onwards accompanied her on all her journeys. This figure, and another portraying the bodyguard of the Empress Alexandra, are said to have been commissioned by Nicholas II in 1912.

Literary Characters

With the exception of an historical figure of a boyar which was probably based on a character from the opera *Boris Godunov*, most of the figures of literary characters seem to have been taken from the West. Fabergé immortalized not only Tweedledum and Tweedledee from Lewis Carroll's *Through the Lookng-Glass*, but also John Bull, Arbuthnot's satirical idea of the Englishman, and Uncle Sam, the personification of America.

All the stone figurines were made in St Petersburg under the supervision of the head workmaster, Henrik Wigström, but the presence of his mark on the silver and gold parts does not mean that he did all the work, including the stone cutting, himself. In St Petersburg initial drawings would be made of a subject (Pustinikov, the *kamerkazak* or bodyguard of the Empress, was ordered to stand and model for Fabergé). Then a wax model would be prepared, based on the drawing. Although the names of several animal modellers are known, no artist can be directly connected with the modelling of the stone figures. Hardstone copies of the wax models were carved and assembled in Karl Woerffels's workshop under the super-

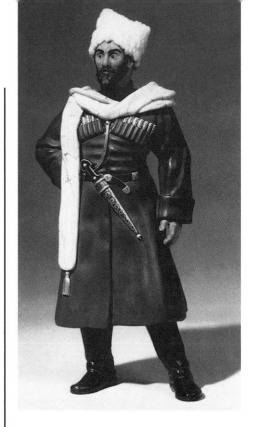

Figure of a cherkess-cossack composed of various hardstones with a cacholong face and cabochon sapphire eyes, a niello dagger on his belt. 22.2 cm (8¾ inches)

vision of Alexander Meier. Artists such as Derbyshev and P. M. Kremlev did the work at this stage.

The individual stones were carved according to the model, then fitted together, glued in place and polished. The different parts were assembled so perfectly that the joints are hardly visible to the naked eye and frequently cannot even be detected with a needle. In order to achieve the intended visual effect careful attention was paid to the natural grain of the stone: Varya Panina's cashmere shawl, for instance, was in speckled jasper. Finally the eyes would be fitted, made of cabochon sapphires or of rose diamonds.

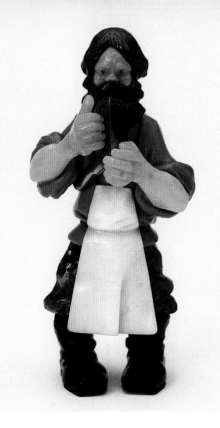

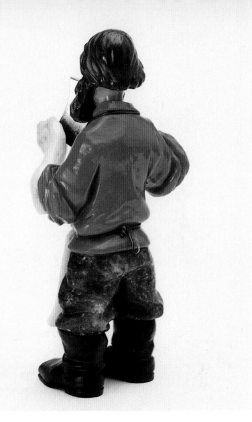

Left: *Carpenter with aventurine quartz face, purpurine shirt and lapis lazuli breeches, testing a gold and silver axe*

Right: *Back view of the carpenter. The engraved Cyrillic signature of Fabergé is under his right foot. 12.7 cm (5 inches) high*

The figures can be divided into two categories according to the stone used for the faces and hands. In the first category they were made of pink, skin-coloured quartz, a relatively hard stone which was carefully carved and polished, resulting in a shiny surface. This group includes the Varya Panina figurine, figures formerly in the Sir William Seeds collection, which included the balalaika player, and the Chelsea Pensioner. In the second category a soft, porous stone, similar to porcelain, was used.

This pale pink stone, which often used to be mistaken for a synthetic composition, consists of a whitish kind of porous opal known as cacholong. Its

relative softness enabled the craftsmen to carve facial features in exact detail, giving the figures a more lifelike appearance. Fabergé used cachalong predominantly after 1913, especially in the figures he made for the Nobels.

Duplicates

Most of the figurines are unique pieces. Duplicates were made only on rare occasions as a result of a special request – and in all such cases Fabergé reserved the right to make slight changes. The John Bull figure, for instance, was repeated several times: but the King of Siam's version had a nephrite jacket, while the one in Sir Charles Clore's collection wears a frock coat made

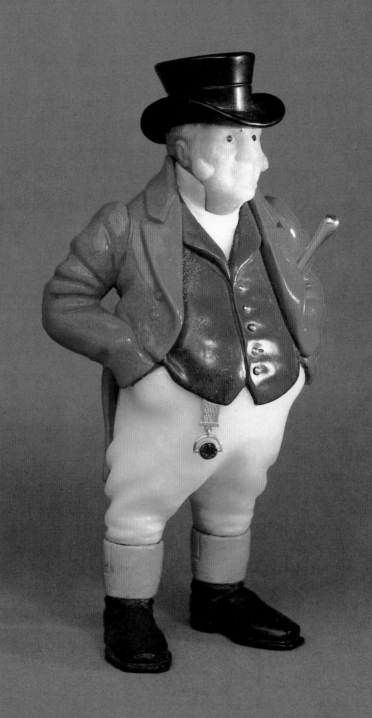

of purpurine. Duplicates exist of the *izvoshchik* or carriage-driver and the painter, and it is thought that Fabergé made a second version of Varya Panina.

Most of the figures are signed under one foot with the name 'FABERGÉ', sometimes with the initial K, in Russian or, more rarely, in Latin script. Sometimes the year and occasionally the inventory number appears engraved on one foot. In addition to the firm's signature, the silver and gold parts were stamped with the initials of the head workmaster, Henrik Wigström, along with the St Petersburg assay mark.

Emanuel Nobel, a Swedish oil industrialist living in Russia and a nephew of Alfred Nobel, owned what was probably one of the largest collections of stone figures before 1918. He and his brother Gustav were among Fabergé's most important customers. Emanuel Nobel is said to have ordered a series of more than 30 stone figures, and many of the ones known today were originally in his possession. One piece made in 1914, a coach driver (*legkovoi*) sitting on a horse-drawn sleigh, is the largest composite hardstone group Fabergé made. The coach driver and sleigh are made of several different kinds of stones and the horse, which has a silver harness, is carved from red-brown quartz.

In the period between 1907 and 1917 only four stone figures were listed in the London sales ledgers:

John Bull, nephrite coat, white onyx waistcoat, yellow orletz trousers, black obsidian hat, boots, gold stick, buttons and watch-chain. Nr. 17099.

27 November 1908, S. Poklewski, £70.

Uncle Sam, white onyx hat, shirt and trousers, obsidian coat, orletz face, grey and red enamel waistcoat, gold watch chain and buttons. Nr. 17714. 10 September 1909, Mrs W. K. Vanderbilt, £60.

Model of a Chelsea Pensioner in pour-pourine, black onyx, silver, gold, enamel, 2 sapphires. Nr. 18913. 22 November 1909, H. M. The King, £49.15s.

Sailor, white onyx, orletz, lapis lazuli, black onyx etc. Nr. 17634. 14 October 1913, Mme Brassow, £53.

The Chelsea Pensioner bought by King Edward VII is still in the Royal Collection. The King of Siam accquired figures of John Bull, a coachman (*likhach*) as well as Tweedledum and Tweedledee, which are all in the royal collection in Bangkok. A figure of a dancing *muzhik* (peasant) and the officer of a Ulan regiment is in the Forbes Magazine collection. The Kremlin Museum houses the figure of a cook which was transferred there from the Imperial collections. A figure of a sailor can be found in the Pratt Collection, Richmond, Virginia, and the Russian girl with purpurine dress and scarf is in the Metropolitan Museum of Art, New York. All other figures are in private collections.

Hardstone figure of John Bull, 12 cm (4¾ inches). Formerly in the Collection of Sir William Seeds

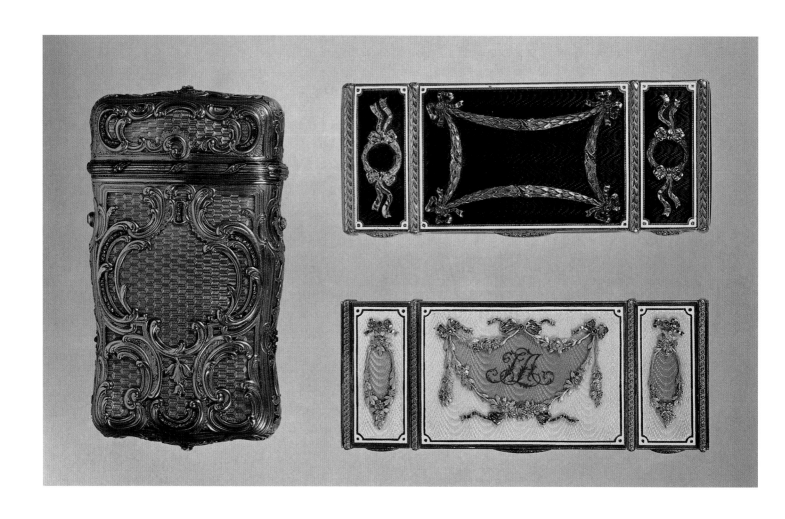

Enamelled gold cigarette case in the Louis XV style by Michael Perchin, and two vanity cases, each with three compartments, by Henrik Wigström

Chapter Six

OBJECTS OF FUNCTION

The Fabergé magic was not restricted to expensive and purely decorative items of jewellery and ornament. Increasingly, from the late 1880s onwards, the Fabergé workshops produced beautiful things which also had practical use. By the 1910s the Fabergé cachet was to be found on a wide variety of otherwise ordinary objects such as penholders, photograph frames, table lighters, ashtrays, cigarette cases, and clocks – the accoutrements of daily life in polite society for home and office. Not all were lavish, ornate or elaborate: but all exhibit that elegance of design, that mastery of materials and techniques, and that perfection of workmanship that make up the Fabergé style.

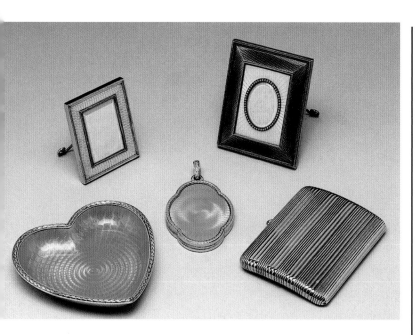

miniatures in silver or gold frames. A number of artists worked for Fabergé painting miniature portraits on ivory. The most famous among them were Johannes Zehngraf (1857–1908) and Vasily Zuiev, who worked for Fabergé from 1908 to 1917.

Around 1890 the hand-held camera was invented and it became the fashion to photograph one's family and friends. Even the members of the Russian Imperial family became fervent amateur photographers and it was evident that frames would be needed for all the

Above left: *Heart-shaped enamelled dish; quatrefoil gold and enamel locket; reeded two-colour gold cigarette case and two small frames*
Below: *Clock of vari-coloured gold and enamel; rock crystal stamp holder and an oriental jade scent bottle*

Clocks, *bonbonnières*, photograph frames, paperknives, seals, penholders, gum bottles, bell pushes, cigarette boxes, ashtrays and pencils are just a few of the many objects of function which Fabergé advertised on a card sent to his London customers in 1907.

Fabergé applied his versatile genius to the production of many kinds of useful objects, but it is their artistic quality and technical perfection which made them so outstanding. Many of these functional objects are illustrated in this book. Two groups, the very popular photograph frames and the clocks, have been singled out for more detailed study in this chapter because they illustrate Fabergé's very high standard of craftsmanship. The same level of stylistic and technical execution can be found in most of the other objects.

Fabergé adopted the 17th and 18th century tradition of mounting painted

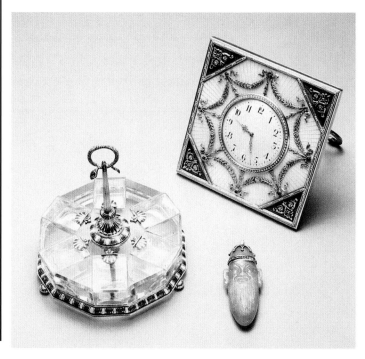

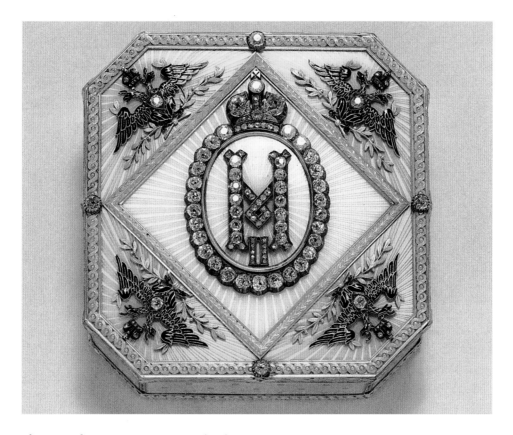

Imperial presentation box enamelled in the Romanov colours and decorated with the crowned cypher of Nicholas II in diamonds

photographs. Interior views of salons and drawing rooms at the turn of the century often show rows of framed portrait photographs on tables, cabinets or on the inevitable grand piano, and they were liberally scattered throughout the rooms. On his desk in his private office Nicholas II had nearly a dozen frames, some of them apparently by Fabergé, with photographs of his mother the Empress Marie Feodorovna and of other members of the imperial family.

The stylistic sources for the decoration of these frames came from earlier periods. The Louis XVI style seems to have been the preferred style for Fabergé frames. They are decorated with flower garlands, laurel crowns, rosettes and elaborate bows, usually on a coloured enamel ground.

Many frames were produced in the Louis XV and Empire styles. Art nouveau frames are comparatively rare. Faberge liked cornflowers and lilies for their decoration and they were enamelled in a technique which combined *guilloché* and *cloisonné* work, as can be seen on the cornflower frame in the Forbes Collection.

The flat surfaces of most frames were decorated with *guilloché* enamel. The *guilloché* technique consists of engine-turning (machine-engraving) a metal

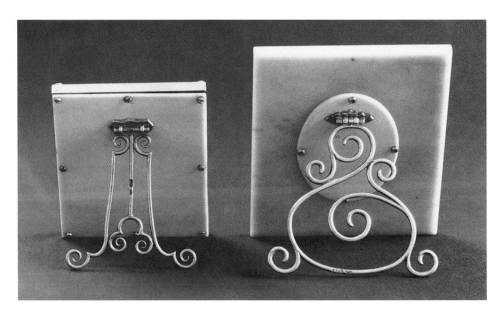

surface with a fine, regular pattern, usually of wavy, parallel, concentric or sunray lines. The pattern would then be covered with separately fired layers of translucent, coloured enamel, the last one normally a transparent gloss enamel to give a brilliant surface finish. The patterns shine through the enamel and sometimes produce moire effects. In some cases the *guilloché* ground has additional decorations of hand-engraved flower garlands which become visible only when lit from a certain angle.

Another decorative effect was achieved by painting subtle patterns such as tree-like motifs or trailing garlands between layers of enamel, which are fired on individually.

The rarest decoration, found only on Faberge's most elaborate objects, consists of ornaments made of gold leaf or *paillons* incorporated into the enamel. Although the enamel workshops in St Petersburg were under the supervision

The backs of Fabergé's frames are covered with ivory and the struts have an unusual decorative shape

of the workmaster Alexander Petrov, this particular technique of enamel with *paillons* was, according to Eugene Fabergé, the work of a Czech named Trasser.

Fabergé's enamel work has become famous for its perfection and for its brilliance and variety of colour. Original colour charts show that up to 144 different basic shades were available. The final brilliance of finish was achieved by long hours of hand-polishing with wooden wheels covered in soft leather.

Guilloché enamel was usually fired on to a silver sheet, though in rare cases, in order to obtain special colour effects such as opalescent pink, it was fired on gold. The borders of the frames could be silver, silver-gilt or gold, cast and chased with ornaments such as palmettes, acanthus or laurel bands. Some particularly decorative flower garlands were made of varicoloured gold; and different alloys of gold with other metals — with copper for red, with silver for green, with nickel or palladium for white — provide naturalistic effects for flowerheads in a garland.

The use of hardstones is also characteristic of Fabergé's frames. He used aventurine, bowenite, rock crystal and, most often, nephrite, which he preferred to all other stones. Nephrite frames are often encrusted with cabochon rubies and rose-cut diamonds. The bezels of some of the more elaborate frames are set with seed pearls.

It was not just the fronts of the frames that were carefully designed and executed; equal attention was paid to the backs. They are covered with thin sheets of ivory fastened with minute screws. Very small frames, only 5cm (2 inches) high, were usually made of gold and have a backing carved from mother-of-pearl: several of these can be found in the Royal collections. The hinged struts are of openwork design and sometimes show interlaced initials or, when the frame was used as an Easter present, the letters X B (Christ is risen).

Most of the frames were made in the St Petersburg workshop under the supervision of the chief workmaster, Michael Perchin or Henrik Wigström, who signed them on the rim as well as on the strut. Another workmaster who specialised in elaborate goldwork and enamel was Victor Aarne. He worked for Fabergé from 1891 to 1904, when his workshop was taken over by his successor Hjalmar Armfelt.

The Moscow branch produced a number of cast silver frames in the rococo or Empire style and also, but more rarely, chased openwork varicoloured gold frames of very high quality. They are signed with only the Imperial warrant mark or the initials КФ: workmasters were not allowed to put their own mark on these objects.

The London sales ledgers record a number of frames. During the financial year 1909–10 the total number of frames sold was 17. The simplest is described as 'Frame, mahogany wood, light green enamel' and was sold

Frame of nephrite and pink enamel with flower garlands in gold of different colours. 2.5 cm (4½ inches) high

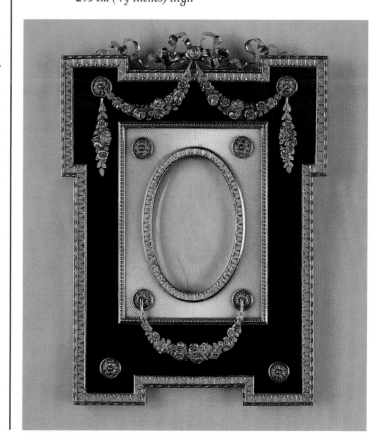

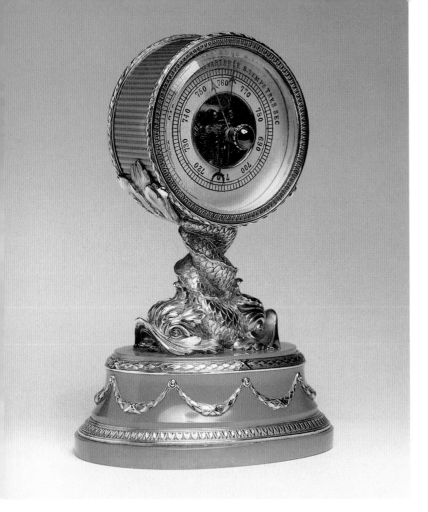

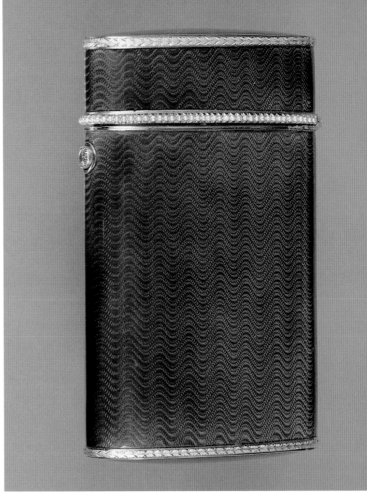

for £5.3s to Mr. Meyer-Sassoon on 14 January 1910. On 29 October 1909 Queen Alexandra bought a 'Frame, blue and red enamel, rim chased in gold' for £70.

Clocks have a special place in Fabergé's *oeuvre*. A Fabergé clock is an *objet d'art* with a practical use – a combination of luxury and function. Decorated in gold, silver, enamel and precious stones, they are the epitome of Fabergé's art. Even some of the famous series of Imperial Easter eggs were made as clocks.

Four examples of these elaborate gifts from Alexander III and Nicholas II to the Empresses are known: The Ser-

Left: *Enamelled barometer held by silver dolphins on a bowenite base by Henrik Wigström. 14 cm (5½ inches)*
Right: *Gold-mounted, enamelled cigarette case of oval section with a diamond catch*

pent Clock Egg (1887, now in an anonymous collection in the USA); the Madonna Lily Egg (1899, now in the Kremlin); the Cuckoo Egg (1900, now in the Forbes Collection, New York); and the Colonnade Egg (1905, now in the Collection of H.M. The Queen). Egg-shaped clocks were also made for the Duchess of Marlborough, Prince Youssoupoff and the Russian gold magnate Alexander F. Kelch.

Most of these ornamental clocks, which conceal their mechanisms within the shell of the egg, have horizontally rotating dials. Only the Cuckoo Egg and the Kelch Chanticleer Egg (Forbes Collection, New York) have the usual round dial with two hands.

Less elaborate, but none the less highly decorative, are the clocks which were made for desks, tables or mantelpieces. These clocks have a dial set into an enamelled, silver, gold or hardstone panel of varying shapes and are decorated in a wide variety of styles.

An Imperial presentation cigarette box of varicoloured gold, enamelled in the Bulgarian royal colours

The most striking are the *guilloché* enamel clocks in colours taken from Fabergé's palette of enamel samples — bright reds and greens or the more subtle shades of pale mauve or opalescent pink.

Stylistically the designs draw mainly on the Louis XVI period, with classical ornaments of architectural friezes decorated with rosettes, garlands and bows. Some clocks are in the rococo style of the Louis XV period with boldly chased scrolls or shells, others in the Empire style with sphinxes, stiff-leaf bands and palmettes. Art nouveau clocks appear to be very rare.

For the hardstone clocks the choice of stone was usually restricted to neph-

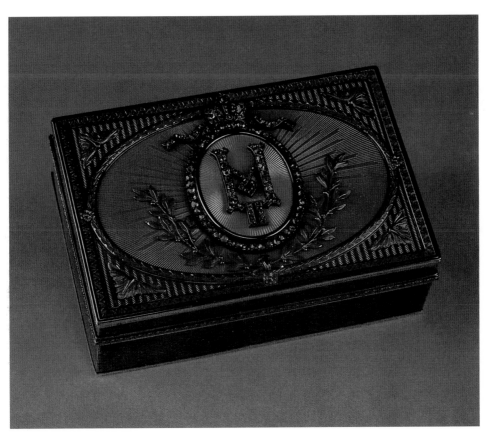

rite – the spinach green variety of Russian jade – pale green bowenite, pink orletz (rhodonite) and dark-blue lapiz lazuli. Styling was much the same as with the enamelled clocks, sometimes combining the hardstone with enamelled motifs or panels. But there are some clocks which seem to anticipate the art deco style. These are more purely functional clocks carved from a block of hardstone such as nephrite.

Nephrite clock with varicoloured gold ornaments set with cabochon rubies and diamonds. 10.5 cm (4⅛ inches) high

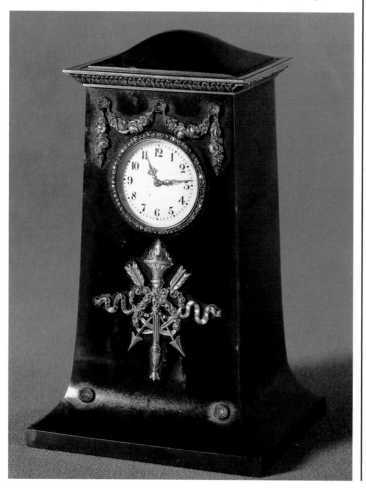

They are very small (about 7.5 cm (3 inches) high) and without decoration apart from the enamelled dial.

Most of the clocks have a standard, opaque white enamel face about 4.5 cm (1½ inches) across. Usually the bezels are decorated with chased laurel or acanthus leaves or are set with seed-pearls. The dials have arabic numerals and the time is shown by openwork gold hands of a standard type. More elaborate clocks have dials with *guilloché* opalescent white enamel on gold which is inscribed *Fabergé* in full. Even rarer are diamond-set numerals on enamelled discs such as those on the Cuckoo Egg and on some strut clocks.

The movements were all imported from Switzerland, made and supplied by the firm of Henry Moser & Cie. of Le Locle. Moser, the founder of the firm, was born in 1803 and came to St Petersburg in 1827 to establish business contacts. He later manufactured clocks in Schaffhausen and Le Locle. After his death the firm continued supplying watches to Russia until 1917.

The movements used for Fabergé's clocks are technically simple nickel-finished bar movements with twin barrel, eight-day lever escapements with compensation balance and using 15 to 17 rubies. Most of them are engraved *Hy. Moser & Cie* and carry a serial number which is also stamped on the Fabergé mount. Another maker of movements is said to have been Paul Buhré. The movements were wound by two fixed keys with folding handles and the backplates bear an engraved Russian inscription indicating an eight-day

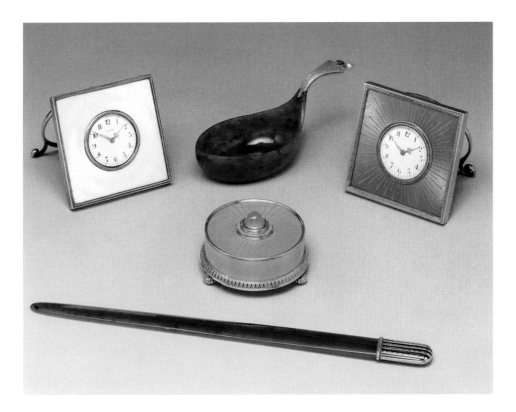

Two enamelled clocks, a nephrite kovsh with enamelled gold mounts, a gold mounted nephrite paperknife and a bell push.

movement (*nedelnyi zavod*). The back is held by a more or less elaborate silver or gold strut.

Only a few chiming clocks are known. Repeating clocks are usually quite large – up to 45 cm (18 inches high) made to sit on a mantelpiece.

Carl Fabergé did not produce any of these clocks himself: his ideas or designs were carried out by the staff of workmasters. Clocks were made principally by the chief workmaster in St Petersburg, Michael Perchin (active 1885/6 to 1903), or his successor Henrik Wigström (1903 to 1918). They signed each piece with their stamped initials. The signature of the firm appears either in an oblong mark or painted in script on the dial. Another workmaster, Julius Rappoport, is known to have made large

silver and silver-gilt mounted mantelclocks or table centrepieces which incorporated clocks. Some unusual examples of clocks were produced by the Moscow branch and bear the mark of Fabergé under the Imperial eagle.

Copies of Fabergé objects are creating a growing problem for the collector today. With clocks, however, the number of forgeries seems to be restricted: the original Swiss movements, dials and hands are too complicated to fake. The danger today lies more in over-restoration or in the use of additions, particularly those intended to suggest an 'Imperial' provenance.

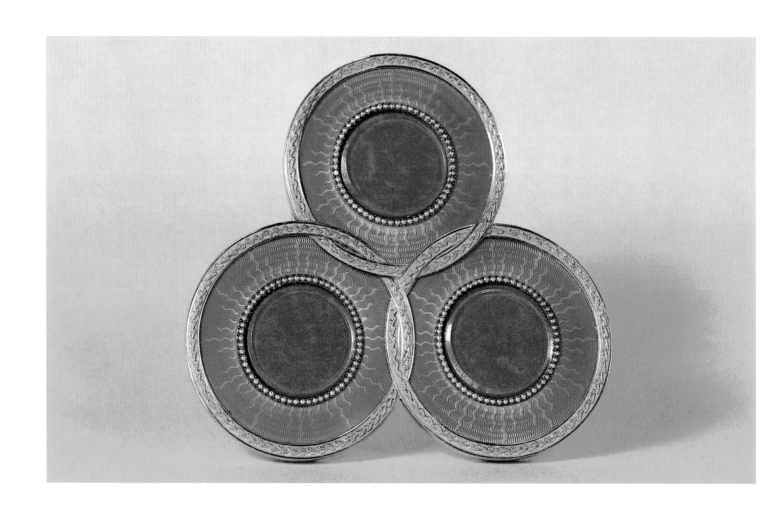

*Triple photograph frame from the collection
of Princess Henry of Prussia. The guilloché
enamel shows an intricate sunburst and
flame pattern in gold mounts by Michael
Perchin*

Chapter Seven

THE HOUSE OF FABERGÉ

The goldsmith's trade may already have been a family tradition when Carl Fabergé's Huguenot ancestors left France in the late 17th century. It was his father, Gustav, who established the family business at St Petersburg. Carl's artistic training and entrepreneurial flair gave the firm the opportunity to develop; his perfectionism, and the patronage of the Tsars, ensured success. By 1900 his customers included royalty and his name and reputation had reached the United States and the Far East. By 1918 war and revolution had closed the company, but many inimitable Fabergé artifacts remain as eloquent testimony to the elegance of life during the belle époque.

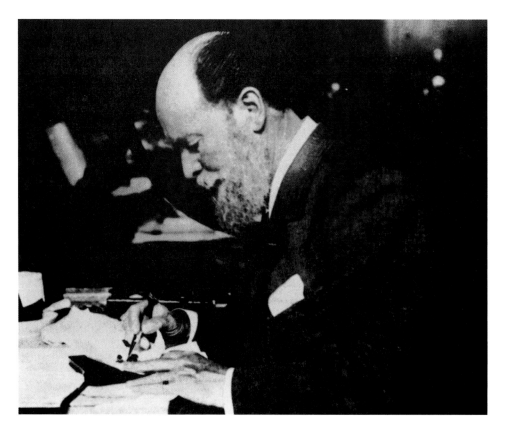

Carl Fabergé sorting precious stones

The Fabergé family can be traced back to the 17th century. French Huguenots, originally called Favri or Fabri, they left France in 1685. After living for several generations in north-eastern Germany under the name of Faberger they settled at Pernau in Estonia which was then part of Russia. Gustav Fabergé, father of Carl, was born here in 1814.

By the 1840s Gustav Fabergé had moved to St Petersburg, then the capital of Russia, where he first studied the goldsmith's art under Andreas Ferdinand Spiegel. Later he joined the firm of Keibel, which in 1826 had remodelled the Rusian crown jewels and in 1842, as a master-jeweller, he set up a business on his own, a jewellery shop in Bolshaya Morskaya Street in the centre of St Petersburg. In the same year he married Charlotte Jungstedt, the daughter of a Danish painter, and on 30 May 1846 their first son, Carl Fabergé, was born. He was christened Peter Carl in the Protestant Church, but in Russian came to be known as Karl Gustavovich.

Carl's education began at St Anne's Gymnasium, the German school in St Petersburg, and he later trained under the goldsmith and jeweller Peter Hiskias Pendin, a friend of his father. The firm's growing prosperity enabled Carl to complete his education abroad. He travelled to Germany, where he was apprenticed to the jeweller Friedmann in Frankfurt am Main, and later to Italy and France, where he completed his art studies with commercial and business training in Paris.

By the time Carl returned to St Petersburg his father had decided to retire from business. He left his firm in the hands of his partner Zaionchkovsky and went to live in Dresden.

Marriage

Shortly afterwards, in 1870, at the age of 24, Carl Fabergé took over the firm under the guidance of his teacher, Hiskias Pendin. In 1872 he married Augusta Julia Jacobs, the daughter of a manager of the Imperial furniture workshops. They were to have four sons: Eugène (1874–1960), Agathon (1876–1951), Alexander (1877–1952) and Nicholas (1884–1939), all of whom eventually joined the firm.

In 1881, the year that the Tsar Alexander II was assassinated (he was succeeded by Alexander III), Hiskias Pendin died. For a year Carl managed the business on his own. Then his younger brother, 20-year-old Agathon, returned from Dresden to join the firm as a jewellery designer. It was Agathon who had the initial idea of producing *objets de fantaisie*, small objects of both artistic and functional value, as opposed to the heavy diamond and gold jewellery which was produced by other Russian jewellers. In 1882 the House of Fabergé exhibited for the first time at the Pan-Russian Art and Industrial Exhibition in Moscow, winning a gold medal for copies of the ancient Greek treasure unearthed at Kerch in the

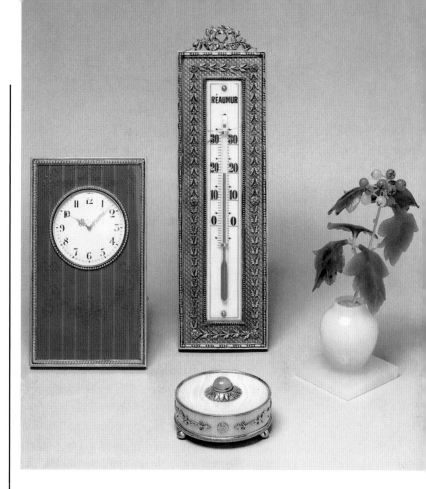

Desk clock by Henrik Wigström, thermometer by Victor Aarne and a flower study of a sprig of hawthorn by Henrik Wigström. The electrical bell push is also by Henrik Wigström

Crimea as well as for other jewellery in the traditional style. This resulted in the first commissions from the Court: in 1883 the name of the firm first appeared in the accounts of His Imperial Majesty's Cabinet.

On 16 April 1885 Fabergé was rewarded with an appointment as Jeweller to the Imperial Court and given the right to have the Imperial Eagle incorporated into the firm's trademark. In the same year, at the request of Tsar Alexander III an Easter Egg was made for Empress Marie Feodorovna. It was the first of a series of 54 lavishly decorated Easter presents which followed over the years until 1916.

1885, was also the first time Fabergé exhibited abroad. At the Exhibition of Applied Arts in Nuremberg he received a gold medal for the replicas of the Kerch treasures made by the chief workmaster of the firm, Erik Kollin. The Nuremberg catalogue describes Fabergé as 'Jeweller to His Majesty and the Imperial Hermitage'.

In 1886 Michael Perchin, a 26-year-old goldsmith jeweller, the son of a peasant from eastern Karelia, joined the house of Fabergé. His outstanding artistic skill soon led to his becoming chief workmaster in succession to Kollin. From then on the firm's production turned away from replicas of ancient jewellery and towards enamelled and jewelled objects – an art which Perchin brought to perfection under Fabergé's guidance.

According to Baron Foelkersam, Fabergé first produced silver in the form of cutlery and tableware in 1887, the year in which a branch of the firm was opened in Moscow. This branch, run in partnership with an Englishman, Allan Bowe, specialized in the production of silverware from the start.

The continuing success of the firm was marked by the award of a special diploma at the Nordic Exhibition in Copenhagen in 1888, and two years later the St Petersburg premises had to be doubled in size. Fabergé was nominated Appraiser of the Imperial Cabinet with the jewellers Zeftigen and Köchli,

and was also decorated with the Order of St Anne, third class.

Commissions and orders were now pouring in and in 1890 Fabergé opened a branch in Odessa. It was a time of economic boom in Russia with growing industrialisation, the building of railroads, and the discovery of oil. All this prosperity was reflected in the growing demand for jewellery and precious objects.

In 1894 Alexander III was succeeded by his son, Nicholas II, who in November married Princess Alix of Hesse-Darmstadt; she became the Empress Alexandra Feodorovna. Nicholas II and the Empress were to be Fabergé's most important clients over a period of more than 20 years.

When Fabergé's brother Agathon, who had been the firm's chief designer, died in 1895 he was succeeded by the Swiss François Birbaum. Eugène Fabergé joined the firm in the same year.

Growing Fame

The coronation of Nicholas II and the Empress Alexandra in 1896 was celebrated with great pomp in Moscow. Fabergé created many items to commemorate this historic event, the most famous being the Imperial Coronation Easter Egg which the Tsar presented to the Empress in 1897. That year Fabergé exhibited at the Nordic Exhibition in Stockholm, where he was granted the Royal Warrant of the Court of Sweden and Norway. By this time his name was identified with goldsmithing of the highest quality and his reputation had spread from Russia to western Europe,

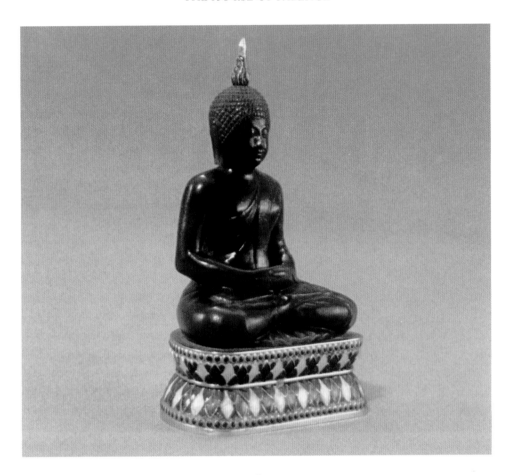

*Buddha meditating by Henrik Wigström.
Fabergé made this figure for a member of
the Thai Royal family. (Collection H.M.
The King of Siam, Bangkok)*

the United States and even to the Far
East where the King of Siam became
one of his customers. The King bought
a large number of items, which are
still kept in the royal collections in
Bangkok.

In St Petersburg larger premises
became necessary. The building at 24
Bolshaya Morskaya Street was acquired
and its reconstruction, under the direction of architect Carl Schmidt, a
nephew of the family, was started in the
same year, 1898. The year 1900 saw the
move to the important new headquarters, which had an imposing granite
façade and which contained not only the
shop premises and most of the work-

shops, but also Fabergé's private
apartments.

The turn of the century was celebrated in Paris with the *Exposition
Universelle*, an exhibition of technical
and artistic achievements from many
parts of the world. Fabergé was represented in the Russian section. At the
request of the Tsar and the Empresses
he exhibited the Imperial Easter eggs,
the miniature diamond-set replica of
the Imperial regalia, and other pieces

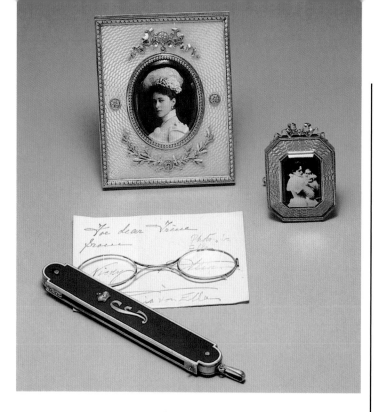

Lorgnette with monogram of the Grand Duchess Elizabeth; a note signed by Nicholas II and Empress Alexandra, and two frames. (Forbes Collection)

such flower studies and jewellery. They were greatly admired both by the public and the judges: Fabergé was made a master of the goldsmith's guild of Paris and decorated with the Cross of the Legion of Honour.

Success at Paris led to a further exhibition of Imperial Eggs in St Petersburg, held at the Palace of Grand Duke Vladimir in 1902.

The London Branch

In 1903 Arthur Bowe, the brother of Allan Bowe, Fabergé's partner in Moscow, started selling pieces in London from his rooms at the Berners Hotel. The first business contacts with English society were taken up and items by

Fabergé were soon on sale at fashionable charity bazaars. In St Petersburg, the chief workmaster, Perchin, died and was succeeded by Henrik Wigström, whose designs were to become famous for their elegant neo-classical French style. He was supervisor of all the workshops until 1918.

A branch was opened in Kiev in 1905, and international business connections were enlarged by Fabergé's visit to Siam. In the following year a shop was opened in London at 48 Dover Street, near the Russian Embassy, under the direction of Nicholas Fabergé and Henry C. Bainbridge.

In 1907 Baron Foelkersam observed in his book *Inventaire de l'Argenterie* that Fabergé ranked amongst the best and most famous jewellers in the world. An article in the magazine *Stolitsa i Usadba* (Town and Country) in January 1914, gave more details. In an interview Fabergé compared himself with Tiffany & Co, Boucheron and Cartier, but said that those firms were merchants, whereas he considered himself an artist-jeweller. The article describes Fabergé's workshops in St Petersburg and Moscow as employing more than 500 workers and designers.

During the First World War, in 1916, the firm was converted into a joint stock company with capital of three million roubles and 600 shares, the majority of which were held by Fabergé and his sons. Due to the war, the workshops produced items in less valuable materials.

In March 1917 Nicholas II was forced to abdicate. Initially kept as prisoners at the palace of Tsarskoe Selo, the Imperial family was taken to Siberia at the end of July. Revolution broke out in St Petersburg in October and the company was taken over by a 'Committee of the Employees of the Company Fabergé', but without the dominating figure of Carl Fabergé production deteriorated. Equally unsurprisingly, the demand for expensive decorative objects had disappeared.

The House of Fabergé finally closed in November 1918. The Imperial family had been assassinated in July and civil war raged throughout Russia. Fabergé decided to emigrate with his family and escaped to the West with the help of the British Embassy. He first settled in Wiesbaden in Germany but in June 1920 moved to Switzerland where he died at the Hotel Bellevue in Lausanne on 24 September.

When the company closed down in 1918 most of the artists and workmasters emigrated, so the death of the great master himself was also the end of the 'Fabergé era'. As an emigré he had been a old and broken man who lacked the stamina and impetus to start again abroad. His four sons had all been trained in the business but it was only Eugène and Alexander who made the effort to build up a new business under the family's famous name.

In 1924 the firm 'Fabergé & Cie.' was registered in Paris, with Eugène and Alexander Fabergé as directors in partnership with Andrea Marchetti, an administrator from the Moscow branch, and Giulio Guerrieri. The objects they produced, however, although most of them were signed Fabergé, were only a dull and remote echo of the originals created in Russia. It was not merely that the perfectionism which Carl Fabergé had been able to maintain so consistently had disappeared: the clientele, the potential market, was taken up by established firms such as Cartier and Lacloche, who were producing jewellery and objects in the new art déco style.

Clock with opalescent enamel plaques, painted en camaïen *with trees, and set in a nephrite frame mounted in varicoloured gold. 10.7 cm ($4\frac{3}{16}$ inches) high*

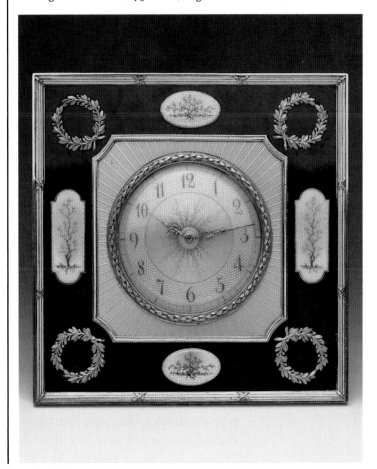

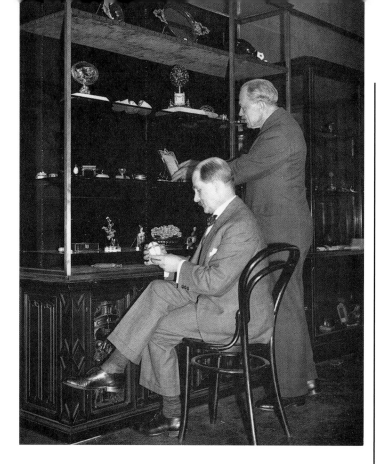

Carl Fabergé's son, Agathon, examines the 1899 Kelch Easter Egg at the 1935 Exhibition of Russian Art in London

The Paris firm worked with enamel as well as hardstones. Eugène Fabergé made contsact with the lapidaries of Idar-Oberstein in Germany, where a number of hardstone objects, especially animals, were produced. In the end, however, the firm's results were disappointing and around 1940 it ceased production.

Alexander Fabergé had started a workshop in Finland, where many of the old workmasters including Henrik Wigström, had settled. Two of Fabergé's grandsons, Theo and Igor, later worked as jewellery designers in Geneva. The firm 'Fabergé & Cie.'

changed hands several times; it still exists in Paris as an establishment specializing in modern jewellery.

Since the 1930s the name 'Fabergé' had been used commercially in the United States by Sam Rubin, originally without the agreement of the Faberge family. In 1951 it was finally agreed that the name could be used, but only for toiletries and perfumes.

Interest in pieces by Fabergé re-emerged with the important exhibition of Russian art in London in 1935. Most of the objects shown came from the collections of the Russian emigré aristocracy and from the English Royal collections. Before the Second World War, however, collectors had been able to acquire items by Fabergé, which were sold by the Soviet Government either directly or through art dealers. Large collections were formed at that time in the United States, including those of Dr Armand Hammer, Lillian Thomas Pratt, India Early Minshall, Matilda Geddings Gray and Marjorie Merriweather Post.

When Soviet government sales stopped after 1945, Fabergé objects became extremely rare. Prices started to rise, and copies and fakes poured on to the market. It is often difficult to decide whether an item is original, since many of the fakes are of high quality.

Valuable information about the history of the firm and its production were first revealed by the manager of Fabergé's London branch, Henry C. Bainbridge, in his study published in 1949. A more substantial work based on pioneering research was written by

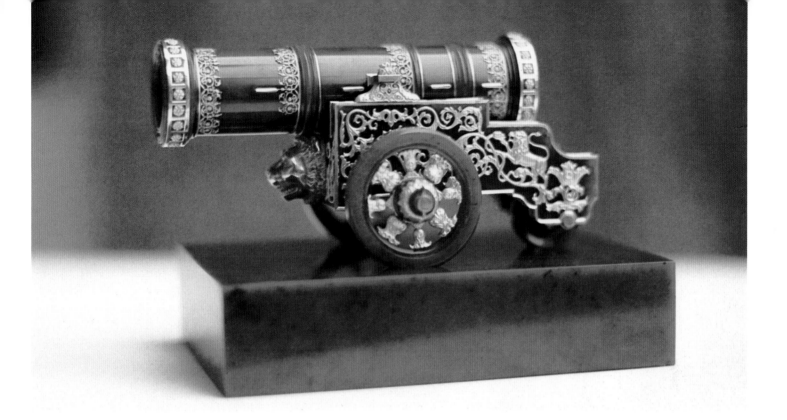

Replica of the Tsar's Cannon from the Kremlin, in gold-mounted nephrite; a gift from Nicholas II to Kaiser Wilhelm II. 17.7 cm (7 inches) long

A. Kenneth Snowman in 1953 and has been revised and reprinted several times. It has become a valuable handbook for the collector.

Since the Fabergé exhibition at the Victoria & Albert Museum in 1977, arranged by A. Kenneth Snowman, the general public has become more interested in Fabergé's work. New, more detailed studies have been written by other authors and specialists. Because of the growing number of fakes exhibitions have become increasingly important, for both collectors and amateurs. Major exhibitions have been held in Helsinki in 1980, in New York in 1983, and at the Queen's Gallery, Buckingham Palace, in London in 1985–6. A comprehensive exhibition showing objects from European royal collections as well as items from the Kremlin Armoury in Moscow and from the

Hermitage in Leningrad was staged in 1986–7 in Munich. In this exhibition Géza von Habsburg focused attention on the use Fabergé made in his *oeuvre* of his knowledge of the history of art and of period styles. The participation of Soviet museums in western European exhibitions seems to have led to growing interest in Fabergé's work in the Soviet Union. Nevertheless American collections seem to be richer in Fabergé objects and Malcom Forbes claims to possess more Imperial Easter eggs than the Kremlin. He recently acquired the Imperial Rosebud egg of 1895, which became the twelfth egg in his collection. The Kremlin has only ten.

LONDON SALES LEDGERS

The sales records of Fabergé's London branch were rediscovered in the late 1970s and provide valuable information about his clientele, production, and prices.

All sales from 6 October 1907 to 9 January 1917 are entered in the ledgers, complete with the date, purchaser's name, description of the item, inventory number, sale price in sterling and cost price in roubles. From 1908 onwards the records were entered by Henry Bainbridge, the manager of the shop.

Easter and Christmas were the best times of the year for sales. These were also the times when a selection of items was taken to France: in December to Paris and in the spring to Nice, Cannes and Monte Carlo. It was most probably Nicholas Fabergé or Henry Bainbridge who delivered the orders, acquired new ones and found new clients.

The last entry was made on 9 January 1917. Although the London branch had officially closed down in 1915 following an Imperial edict that all capital abroad should be returned to Russia for the financing of the war, Bainbridge apparently carried on selling without restrictions.

Hundreds of names are listed in the ledgers. Fabergé's clientele were the most fashionable and wealthy of Edwardian society, most notably King Edward VII and Queen Alexandra themselves. Their visits to the shop were not particularly frequent, but they usually bought quite a number of items and many of them can still be found in the Royal collections today. The ledger records, for example: 'Frame, nephrite, painted enamel view of Sandringham $\frac{1}{2}$pearls, Nr. 17651', bought by the Queen for £52.10s. on 14 January 1909.

All those in the King's immediate circle of friends, and who therefore epitomised Edwardian society, are mentioned as clients who regularly visited the shop. They included the Hon. Mrs. George Keppel, Sir Ernest Cassel, Earl Howe, Lady Arthur Paget, the Duchess of Roxburghe, Lady Cooper and the Hon. Mrs. Ronald Greville. Mrs. Greville bought the hardstone figure of the King's favourite dog 'Caesar' on 28 November 1910. Other London customers were Lady Sackville, the Maharajah of Bikanir, Viscountess Curzon, the Empress Eugenie, the Queens of Italy and Spain, King Manuel of Portugal, the Dowager Empress of Russia and the Prince Aga Khan.

Coronation Vase

Leopold de Rothschild, one of the great patrons of Fabergé's London branch, visited the shop regularly and placed large orders. They included the Coronation Vase, described in the ledgers as 'Cup, rock crystal, engraved gold 72°, enamel, different stones, Nr.

Enamelled two-colour gold clock, the dial with painted opalescent white guilloché enamel, by Henrik Wigström

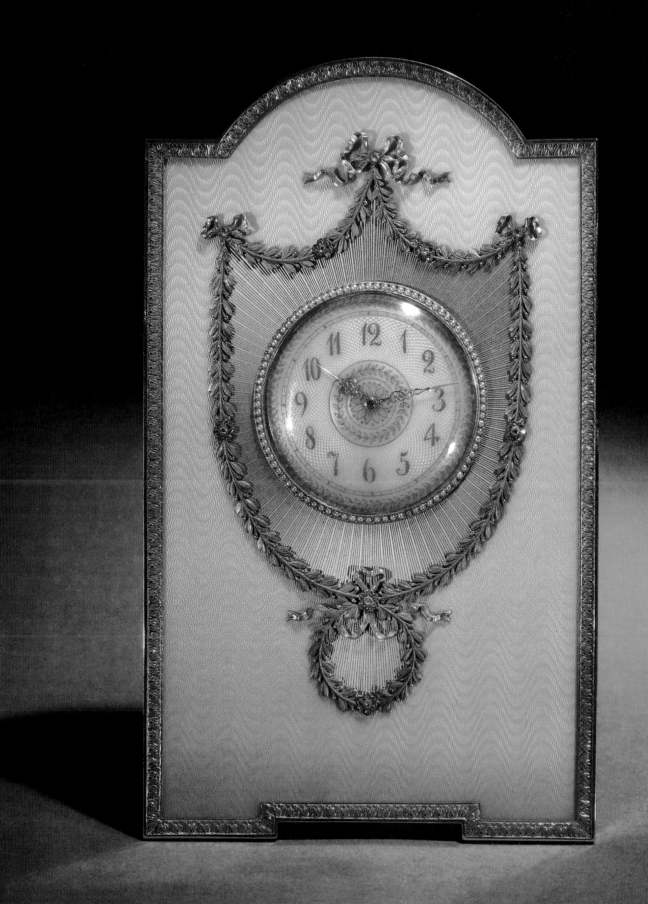

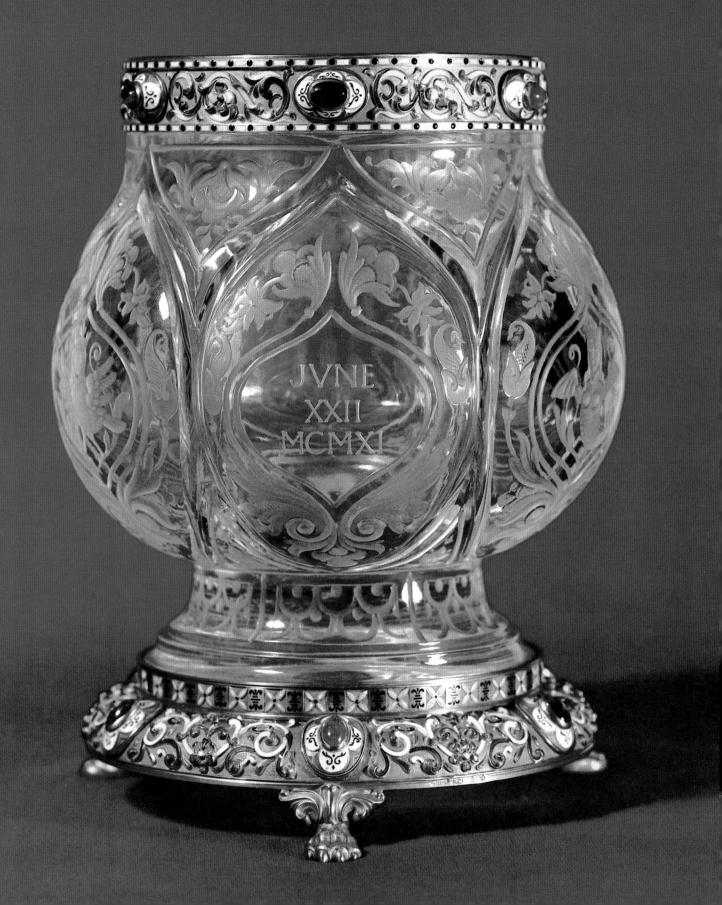

18011', and bought for £430 on 12 April 1911. He gave this vase to King George V and Queen Mary at their coronation filled with orchids from his gardens in Gunnersbury. On 7 December 1911 he bought a *bonbonnière* in 'blue and yellow striped enamel', the Rothschild racing colours, which can be found on a number of objects.

The descriptions of the objects are short but precise, and specify the materials used as well as the colours of the enamels. Apart from the famous clocks, boxes, frames and miniature Easter eggs there are also more unusual objects recorded which show the extraordinary versatility of Fabergé's craftmanship. There are, for example, 'clinical thermometers and crochet hooks'.

Sales Breakdown

A few statistics give an idea of the firm's production. Between 1907 and 1917 nearly 10,000 pieces were sold. From 14 July 1912 to 13 July 1913, the accounting year, a total of 713 objects were sold. The breakdown is interesting. There was a surprisingly large number of cigarette cases, a total of 91 altogether; 71 miniature Easter eggs, 25 animal figures, 23 photograph frames, and eight desk clocks, were amongst items sold during the period. The rarest items of all are the flower studies and the stone figurines.

In the ledgers the description of an

Rock crystal vase in the Renaissance style, by Michael Perchin, which Leopold de Rothschild presented to King George V and Queen Mary at their coronation

object is followed by its inventory number. Every piece has such a number and it is usually found scratched on the metal base, near the signature. Hardstone objects, especially the animal figures which are usually unsigned, have a number in the sales ledgers, but do not have a number marked on them. The same is true of the miniature Easter eggs and the smaller pieces of jewellery, on which even the stamp would hardly be visible owing to lack of space. Occasionally the inventory numbers can be found on the wooden cases, either scratched or written in ink. Most items in the London inventory had numbers between 11,000 and 24,000, although not all numbers are traceable in the ledgers.

Fabergé's luxury objects were always relatively expensive. The 713 objects which are mentioned in the ledgers for the year 1912–13 sold for a total of £16,401.

Miniature Easter eggs in simple enamel cost from 10s. to £1, gold mounted Easter eggs from £3 to £10; silver cigarette cases, £7 to £20; enamel cigarette cases, £21 to £40; hardstone cigarette cases, £35 to £80; and gold ones from £63 to £120. Mounted wooden photograph frames cost £4 to £7 and enamel frames £20 to £30. Table clocks ranged from £27 to £70 depending on the work involved. The average price for hardstone animal figures was £25.

Flower studies cost between £20 and £117 and the hardstone figurines from £49 to £70. The most expensive objects were items of jewellery where the materials themselves were of high in-

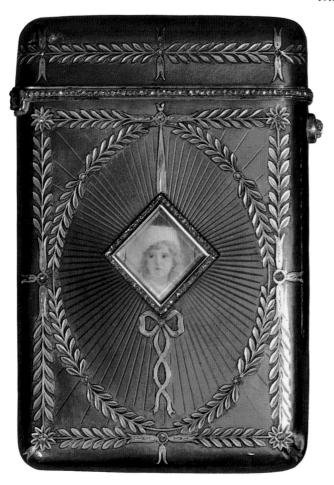

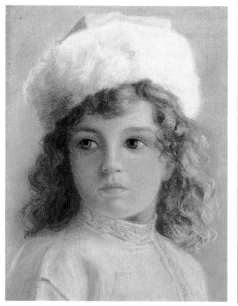

trinsic value like the diamond tiara sold to Mrs. Wrohan in 14 December 1909 for £1,400.

These prices need to be seen in relation to the value of money at the time. According to the 1911 Baedeker guide to London a room at Claridge's Hotel and an à la carte dinner at the Ritz both cost about half a guinea (a guinea was one pound and one shilling). The salary of a Fabergé jewellery designer was 160 roubles or £17 a month, according to Allan Bowe, the director of Fabergé's Moscow branch, in a letter dated 1901.

The last column in the sales ledgers records the cost price of each item of roubles and shows that the profit margin was calculated at about 80 to 100 per cent. A number of items, however, were sold at net prices. These were often objects commissioned by favourite customers.

Above left: *Imperial cigarette case of engraved gold with blue enamel, set with a miniature portrait of the Tsarevitch Alexei, 1907 (Armoury Museum, The Kremlin, Moscow)*
Below left: *Portrait of the Tsarevitch in pastels which the Empress kept in her bedroom at the Alexander Palace in Tsarskoe Selo*
Opposite: *A page from Fabergé's London sales ledgers recording purchases made by Queen Alexandra and her sister, Empress Marie, on Christmas Eve, 1912*

Date.	Customer's Name.	Description of Goods.	Stock Number.	Selling Price.			S. L. Folio.	Cost Price.	
				Details.	Total.				
				£ s. d.	£ s. d.			Rbls. Cop.	
1912		Bforward			£ 1851·14 · ·			10,429.99	
Dec									
24	Wm Koch	Brooch, 1 star sap: roses	91195	10 10 · ·				55	
		Pendant, mecca, wht. enl.	93920	10 · · ·				53	
		Frame, wht. maple; silvr	52310	5 15 · ·				31	
		Tiepin, chryso & red enl.	94141	4 10 · ·	30·15 · ·	331		22	
1	Queen Alexandra	Bracelet, sil. 2 moons, roses	95221	15 · · ·				75	
		Do platinum; gold	9670	12 10 · ·				78	
		Fan, lt. blue en: gold mts.							
		rornts. rubies; white opl.	17524	26 · · ·				118	
		Links, 4 blue meccas, plat.	95199	14 · · ·				80	
		Elephant, pow pow cine	22693	11 15 · ·	79 5 · ·	1		55	
1	Dow. Empress	Pendant, 1 ameth: diads	91102	27 · · ·				141	
	Marie of Russia	Pencil & cutter, blue enl.	21774	5 5 · ·				31	
		Locket, st. blue enl. 1 brill.	95826	8 15 · ·	41 · · ·	5		49	
1	Mrs Cole	Tiepin, gold 56; 1 neph:							
	(Sandringham.)	cab. white opg. enamel	10838	gratis	· · ·	1		22	
26	G. Duke Michael	Neck ornt brills & roses							
		mtd. on black silk rib: &c		nett 120 · · ·	311			855	
1	King Manuel	Cig. case, oval, lt. pink enl.	22842	22 · · ·	375			112	
27	A. S. Vagliano	Links, gold, 4 sap. cab. brills	91791	36 10 · ·				185	
		Do, 4 sap cab; diads.	73708	57 · · ·				335	
		Buttons, (4) wht. opl. enl.							
		& roses (part of set)	95832	8 8 · ·	101·18 · ·	31		46	
		Bforward			£ 2246·12 ·	R. 12,712.99			

REFERENCE SECTION

SIGNATURES AND HALLMARKS

Marks on Fabergé items include various types of signatures, the workmasters' initials and the hallmarks of St Petersburg or Moscow. They give the proof of a genuine piece and allow the dating within a certain number of years.

The Hallmarks

These marks guaranteed that an item was made of precious metal. The Russian gold and silver standards were reckoned in zolotniks – 96 zolotniks correspond to 24-carat gold and to pure silver. The most frequently found proportions for silver alloys are 84 and 88 zolotniks; objects with 91-zolotnik marks were often made for export. These standards correspond to 875, 916 and 947/1000 respectively, while sterling silver is 925/1000. For gold the Russian standard marks are 56 and 72 zolotniks, corresponding to 14- and 18-carat gold.

Moscow

Objects made in the Moscow workshop are marked K. Fabergé in Cyrillic characters, together with the double-headed eagle in one punch

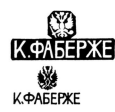

Fabergé's initials in Cyrillic characters for small objects

St Petersburg

Fabergé's full signature (without initial) in Cyrillic characters

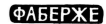

Silver objects from the workshops of Nevalainen, Rappoport, Wäkevä and the First Silver *Artel* (ICA) have the signature in Cyrillic with the initial K. and the Imperial Warrant in a separate punch

Fabergé's initials in Cyrillic characters for small objects

Objects, usually made for export, can be marked with Fabergé's full name or his initials in Roman letters

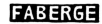

	St Petersburg	Moscow
Late 19th century (until 1899)	56 Ж	Л.О 1894 88
1899–1908	56	84
1908–1917	α 72	Δ 88

Fabergé Workmasters and their Marks

 Johan VICTOR AARNE (1863–1934), born in Finland; Fabergé workmaster from 1891 to 1904. After selling his workshop to Hjalmar Armfeldt in 1904 he opened his own workshop in Viipuri, Finland. His signature is to be found on gold and silver articles, often enamelled. He specialized in picture frames and bellpushes.

 FEDOR AFANASSIEV made small articles of high quality in enamel: miniature Easter eggs, small frames, and cigarette cases. His mark appears in the hallmarking period 1899–1908. No further dates of his life are known.

 Karl Gustav HJALMAR ARMFELT (1873–1959), born in Finland, workmaster under Anders Nevalainen from 1895 until 1904. Studied at the German art school at St Petersburg 1887–89 and and at Baron Stieglitz's school for applied arts 1889–1904. In 1904 he bought the workshop of Victor Aarne and became workmaster for Fabergé on the recommendation of Aarne and Nevalainen. He mainly produced enamelled objects for Fabergé until 1916. Armfeldt emigrated to Finland, where he worked from 1920 on.

AΓ ANDREJ GORIANOV took over from Reimer after his death in 1898. He specialized in small gold and enamel objects and cigarette cases. They bear only his mark, not Fabergé's.

 AUGUST Frederik HOLLMING (1854–1913), born in Finland, workmaster in St Petersburg from 1880 until his death, with a workshop at 35 Kazanskaya Street; in 1900 he moved into Fabergé's new building. For Fabergé he produced gold and silver boxes and ornaments, some of them enamelled. Occasionally he made small enamelled jewellery.

His son, August Väinö Hollming (1885–1934), ran his father's workshop from 1913 until 1918.

Fabergé's signature on a silver item made by workmaster, Julius Rappoport, whose initials IP appear together with the St Petersburg hallmark

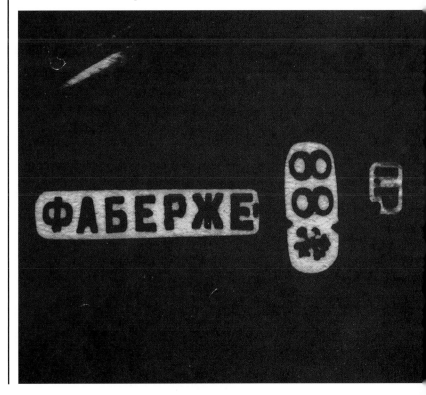

AUGUST Wilhelm HOLMSTRÖM (1829–1903), born in Helsinki, workmaster in 1857 with his own workshop. Senior member of Fabergé's firm; he was head jeweller.

His son, ALBERT Woldemar HOLMSTRÖM (1876–1925), took over the workshop at his father's death in 1903 and continued to work in St. Petersburg until 1918; later in Finland. He used the same mark as his father.

One daughter, Hilma Alina, worked as a jewellery designer for Fabergé.

ERIK August KOLLIN (1836–1901), born in Finland, qualified as work-

The Imperial warrant mark with the double-headed eagle above the name KFABERGE; this mark was used by the Moscow workshop. The Moscow silver hallmark for 1896 appears below and the inventory number is scratched on the right

master in 1868; in 1870 opened his own workshop in St Petersburg at 9 Kazanskaya Street. Kollin worked exclusively for Fabergé, and was soon put in charge of all Fabergé workshops, a post he held until 1886 when he was succeeded by Michael Perchin. He specialized in gold and silver articles. The replicas of the Scythian Treasures, exhibited at the 1885 Nuremberg Exhibition, were made in his workshop.

Karl GUSTAV Johansson LUNDELL (1833–?) is not recorded as qualified master, but worked for Fabergé's Odessa branch. His mark rarely appears together with that of Fabergé's.

ANDERS MICKELSSON (1839–1913), born in Finland, was a master goldsmith and jeweller by 1867. He produced mainly gold cigarette cases and small enamelled objects.

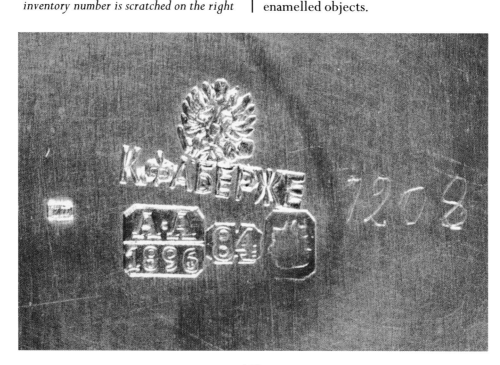

ANDERS Johan NEVALAINEN (1858–1933), born in Finland, became master in 1885. He worked exclusively for Fabergé, first in August Holmström's workshop, then independently in his own. He made small articles in gold and silver, including enamelled frames and cigarette cases, and was also a specialist in mounting wooden and ceramic objects in silver.

GABRIEL Zachariasson NIUKKANEN, master between 1898 and 1912 with his own workshop in St Petersburg at 39 Kazanskaya Street. He made plain gold cigarette cases, which only on occasion bore Fabergé's signature.

MICHAEL Evlampievich PERCHIN (1860–1903), born in Petrozavodsk, Eastern Karelia, died in St Petersburg. Perchin, Fabergé's legendary workmaster, was head of the workshops from 1886 until his death. His workshops was at 11 Bolshaya Morskaya Street until 1900 when he moved to Fabergé's new premises at number 24. His workshop produced all types of *objets de fantaisie* in gold, enamel, and hardstones. He was responsible for the Imperial Easter Eggs made between 1886 and 1903.

He used two punches: one rectangular, one oval, which both appear on the 1897 Coronation Easter Egg. His rectangular mark was probably used from 1886 until 1895, and the oval punch was applied from 1895 to 1903.

Knut OSKAR PIHL (1860–1897), born in Finland, workmaster in 1887, manufactured small jewellery pieces. He was the chief jeweller at Fabergé's Moscow branch between 1887 and 1897. He married Fanny Florentina, a daughter of August Holmström.

Pihl's daughter, Alma Teresia Pihl (1888–1976), started as a jewellery designer in the workshop of her uncle, Albert Holmström. She made the designs of the 1913 Winter Egg and the 1914 Mosaic Egg.

His son Oskar Woldemar Pihl (1890–1959) was a workmaster and jewellery designer in Holmström's workshop from 1913. After 1918 he (eventually) joined the Tillander firm in Helsinki.

The Fabergé signature, the initials of the workmaster, Henrik Wigström and the St. Petersburg kokoshnik hallmark and the inventory number. These marks appear on an enamelled gold clock.

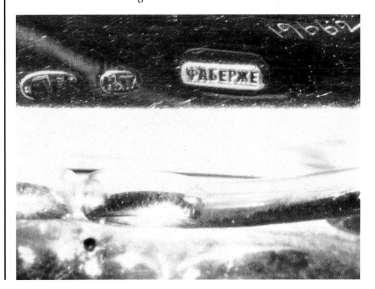

I.P. JULIUS Alexandrovich RAPPOPORT (1864–1916) had his own workshop at Ekatarininski Canal from 1883, where he remained when Fabergé moved his staff to the house in Bolshaya Morskaya Street. Rappoport was head silversmith and produced large objects and services, as well as silver animals.

W.R WILHELM REIMER (died c. 1898), born in Pernau. Made small enamel and gold objects.

T.R Philip THEODOR RINGE had his own workshop from 1893 on, where he made objects in enamelled gold or silver.

Ф.P. FEDOR RÜCKERT, born in Moscow, of German origin. He started making objects with *cloisonné* enamel in Moscow in 1877. Fabergé's Moscow signature often obliterates Rückert's initials.

Rückert also sold his *cloisonné* objects independently, which explains why a number of his pieces bear no Fabergé signature.

ES EDUARD Wilhelm SCHRAMM, born in St Petersburg, of German origin, worked for Fabergé before 1899 making cigarette cases and gold objects; in most instances he signed only with his own initials.

BC VLADIMIR SOLOVIEV took over Ringe's workshop after his death, and made similar objects. His initials can often be found under the enamel on pieces made for export to England.

The marks which appear on the cigarette case illustrated on page 8: the London import mark for 1913, the initials CF, the inventory number and the kokoshnik hallmarks and HW for Henrik Wigström

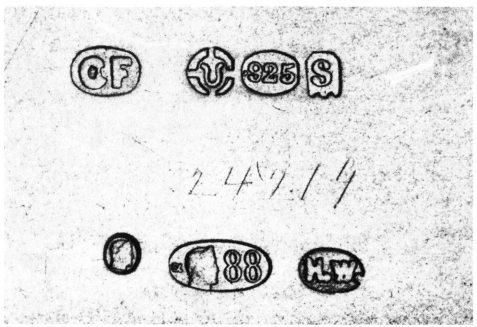

ALFRED THIELEMANN (date of birth unknown, died between 1908 and 1910), of German origin, master from 1858 and active as jeweller for Fabergé from 1880. Thielemann produced trinkets and small pieces of jewellery; his place was taken after his death by his son, Karl Rudolph Thielemann.

The mark AT was also used by three other masters who did not work for Fabergé: Alexander Tillander produced objects in the style of Fabergé. A. Tobinkov was a workmaster in the firm of silversmiths Nicholls & Plincke; the third was A. Treiden.

 STEFAN WÄKEVÄ (1833–1910), born in Finland, master in 1856. He made silver articles for practical use.

His son, ALEXANDER WÄKEVÄ (1870–1957), was trained as a silversmith with his father and took over the workshop in 1910.

 HENRIK Immanuel WIGSTRÖM (1862–1923), born in Taminisaari, Finland. In 1886 he obtained a post as journeyman with Michael Perchin After Perchin's death in 1903 Wigstrom became Fabergé's head workmaster until 1917. The Imperial Easter Eggs were made under his direction from 1904 to 1916. Nearly all hardstone animals, figurines, and flowers were produced under his supervision as well as frames, etuis and *objets de vitrine* of high quality made of gold, hardstone and enamel.

His son, Henrik Wilhelm Wigström (1889–1934), was apprenticed to his father and worked with him until 1917.

The First Silver *Artel*, a cooperative of independent jewellers, goldsmiths, and silversmiths, worked for Fabergé between 1890 and 1917, producing silver articles including animals and a number of objects in *guilloché* enamel.

There are other unidentified workmasters' marks appearing in conjunction with Fabergé's signature, for example:

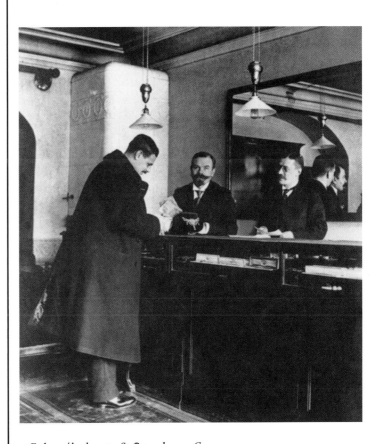

Fabergé's shop in St Petersburg. George Stein, the workmaster who made the miniature carriage for the Coronation Coach Egg of 1897 is in the centre

GLOSSARY

bonbonnière: a small container for sweets

bibelot: a trinket or curio

bowenite: a Russian serpentine of a pale, milky green colour

boyar: a member of an old order of Russian nobility. The order, abolished by Peter the Great, came just below the princes in order of rank.

bratina: a Russian punchbowl

brilliant-cut diamond: a circular-cut diamond with a flat top

briolette-cut: (of a gem) pear-shaped and with long triangular facets

cabochon: a precious stone domed and polished but not faceted

cacholong: (also Kascholong) a white, enamel-like variety of opal

chased: (of metal) ornamented by engraving or embossing

cloisonné enamel: enamel melted into compartments formed by thin strips of metal fastened to a flat metal surface

collet mount: a collar-like band of metal holding an individual stone

commesso: the technique of combining in a single sculpture stones of different colours, patterns and textures

en ronde bosse enamel: enamel covering a curved surface or relief

finial: an end-decoration; an ornament at the top of a cover or at an apex

foiled: (of a gem) having a thin piece of highly reflective metal, often gold or silver leaf, set behind it to bring out its colour and brilliance

grisaille: monochrome painting in shades of grey

guilloché enamel: translucent, coloured enamel covering a machine-engraved metal surface

ittobori: (literally 'one-cut carving') a simple, folk-art style of Japanese netsuke carving which can result in a geometric and formalized appearance

jetton: a circular or tablet-like counter of the kind used for gambling games such as roulette

kitsch: ('trash, rubbish') a tawdry, vulgar or pretentious work (usually of art, sometimes literature or music) often with popular appeal from being cute or sentimental

Kunstkammer: originally a small room, later sometimes a cupboard or showcase, for keeping and displaying small curios, rarities, precious artefacts and natural curiosities (see also *Wunderkammer*)

labradorite: a darkish hardstone named after Labrador, where it is found, with sometimes striking colour-change effects of blues and greens

lubok: moralising picture-stories, usually in woodcuts, popular in Russia in the 18th and 19th century

Mecca stone: a cabochon chalcedony stained pink or blue

moiré: having a wavy, reflective, slightly changing pattern characteristic of a water-treated fabric

nécessaire: a small, portable box or case made to hold certain specific items or equipment

nephrite: a variety of jade, of a spinach green shade

netsuke: (literally 'root-fixing') a toggle or toggles, usually made from wood, jade, ivory or lacquer. A cord passed through a hole in a netsuke enabled an item to be carried by hanging it from the sash of a kimono

objets de fantaisie: objects of capricious, eccentric, or unusually fanciful design or manufacture

objets de vitrine: showcase pieces; small, precious objects usually forming a collection for display

obsidian: dark and coloured vitreous volcanic rock

paillons: small pieces of metal e.g. silver or gold leaf, used with enamel

plique-à-jour enamel: a form of *cloisonné* enamel without the backing; with translucent enamels the technique gives a stained-glass effect

portrait diamond: a table-cut diamond

purpurine: an artificial 'stone' made of fused glass of a deep red colour

rhodonite: (a Russian orletz) a vitreous, pearly, translucent hardstone occurring in various shades of pink to red

rock crystal: transparent quartz, normally found in sedimentary rocks such as limestones

rose diamond: (sometimes rose-cut diamond) a diamond, usually a small one, with the top cut into triangular facets

sagemono: (literally 'hanging things') anything carried by being suspended from the sash of a kimono

satuarn: a form of aventurine, a red-brown or sometimes green hardstone, vitreous, translucent, and with a metallic glint or iridescence

table-cut diamond: a thin, rectangular diamond cut with a flat top surface like a table

torque: a neckband or armband, usually made of twisted metal

Wunderkammer: (literally 'chamber of marvels') originally a room in a palace or large house in which curiosities, rarities, strange, freakish, or precious objects and works of art were kept for admiration. Modern museums of various kinds have their origins in such collections

---

COLLECTIONS

The museums and galleries listed below contain sizeable collections of Faberge's work which are open to the public. The English Royal Collection is not on permanent view, but items are occasionally lent for exhibitions at the Queen's Gallery, Buckingham Palace Road, London, SW1, and at other museums.

Great Britain
Wernher Collection
Luton Hoo
Park Street
Luton
Bedfordshire

United States of America
Forbes Magazine Collection
60 Fifth Avenue
New York
New York 10011

India Early Minshall Collection
Cleveland Museum of Art
11150 East Boulevard
Cleveland
Ohio 44106

Lillian Thomas Pratt Collection
Virginia Museum of Fine Arts
Boulevard and Grove Avenue
Richmond
Virginia 23221

Marjorie Merriweather Post Collection
Hillwood Museum
Washington
D.C.

The Walters Art Gallery
600 N. Charles Street
Baltimore
Maryland 21201

USSR
Armoury Museum
The Kremlin
Moscow

BIBLIOGRAPHY

Books

Bainbridge, Henry C: *Peter Carl Fabergé*, London, 1949. New edition, 1966

Habsburg-Lothringen, Géza, von, and Solodkoff, Alexander von: *Fabergé: Court Jeweller to the Tsars*, London, 1979

Ross, Marvin: *The Art of Carl Fabergé and his Contemporaries*, Oklahoma, 1965

Snowman, A. Kenneth: *The Art of Carl Fabergé*, London, 1953. Revised and enlarged edition, 1962

Snowman, A. Kenneth: *Carl Fabergé: Goldsmith to the Imperial Court of Russia*, London, 1979

Solodkoff, Alexander von: *Masterpieces from the House of Fabergé*, New York, 1984

Solodkoff, Alexander von: *Fabergé Clocks*, London, 1986

Waterfield, Hermione and Forbes, Christopher: *Fabergé: Imperial Eggs and Other Fantasies*, London, 1979

Articles in Periodicals

Bainbridge, Henry C: 'Russian Imperial Easter Gifts', *The Connoisseur*, V, VI, 1934

Forbes, Christopher: 'Imperial Treasures', *Art and Antiques*, IV, 1986

Habsburg-Lothringen, Géza von: 'Fabergé, – ein Plagiator?', in *Kunst und Antiquitaten*, II, 1987

Lopato, Marina: 'Fresh Light on Fabergé', *Apollo*, I, 1984

Munn, Geoffrey: 'Fabergé and Japan', *Antique Collector*, I, 1987

Snowman, A. Kenneth: 'Two Books of Revelations', *Apollo*, IX, 1987

Solodkoff, Alexander von: 'Fabergé's London Branch', *The Connoisseur*, II, 1982

Solodkoff, Alexander von: 'Fabergé Animals', *Antique Collector*, IX, 1987

Württemberg, Alexander Herzog von: 'Glanz und Hohepunkt der Russischen Hofkunst, in *Weltkunst*, III, 1987

Exhibition Catalogues

Fabergé, 1846–1920. International Loan Exhibition on the occasion of the Silver Jubilee, 1977. (Illustrated catalogue compiled by A. Kenneth Snowman)

Fabergé at Hillwood (compiled by Katrina V. H. Taylor), Washington D.C., 1983

Carl Fabergé and his Contemporaries, Tillander, Helsinki, 1980

A Souvenir Album of Fabergé from the Royal Collection, Queen's Gallery, 1985

Fabergé (compiled by Géza von Habsburg), Munich, 1986. English edition, Geneva, 1987

INDEX

ACKNOWLEDGEMENTS

An expression of gratitude is due to the following persons and institutions for their kind help in supplying photographic material and information for this book:

H.M. Queen Elizabeth II
H.M. The Queen of Denmark
H.M. The King of Thailand
H.R.H. The Duchess of Mecklenburg
H.R.H. Princess Eugénie of Greece and Denmark
H.R.H. Dr. Alexander Duke of Württemberg
H.H. George Alexander Duke of Mecklenburg

Michael Becher, Mr. and Mrs. Lyon Boston, Tatjana Fabergé, Christopher Forbes, John Gaze and Christopher Martin (Iconastas), Dr. Géza von Habsburg-Lothringen, Julia Harland (Lord Chamberlain's Office), Jørgen Hein (Rosenborg Museum), Alice M. Ilich (Christie's), Margaret Kelly, Khunying Busaya Krairiksh, Nicholas Lynn (Winter Palace), Countess M. M. Mordvinoff, Geoffrey C. Munn, Katharina Schliemann (Sotheby's), Martin Schwartz, A. Kenneth Snowman (Wartski), Dr. Fabian Stein (Ermitage Ltd.), Ulla Tillander, Katrina V. H. Taylor (Hillwood Museum).

The author and the publishers like to thank the following for their kind help in supplying illustrations:
Ahmet Arkun: 17; Armoury Museum, The Kremlin, Moscow: 27, 36, 42, 114; BBC Hulton Picture Library: 108; Brooklyn Museum, Bequest of Helen B. Saunders: 65; Christie's, Geneva: 8, 19, 21, 24, 62, 71, 78, 79, 84, 88, 90, 95, 97, 100; De Danske Kongers Kronologiske Samling, Rosenborg Castle: 98; Ermitage Ltd: 10, 11, 15, 20, 48, 49, 50, 52, 53, 59, 73, 74, 75, 76, 77, 80, 83, 86, 92, 94, 96, 99, /Prudence Cuming Associates Ltd: 103, 107, 111, 115; Fabergé Archive: 6, 30, 43, 102; Forbes Magazine Collection (H. Peter Curran, Peter McDonald, Larry Stein): 2, 9 (inset), 13, 14, 16, 20, 23 (inset), 25, 28, 29, 32, 35, 37, 38, 41, 45, 57, 58, 91, 92, 106; Matilda Geddings Grey Foundation, on loan to the New Orleans Museum of Art: 26, 60; The Hillwood Museum, Washington D.C.: 33; Iconostas: 18; Octopus Publishing Group: 40, 64; James Ogilvy: 51; Royal Collection, reproduced by gracious permission of H.M. The Queen: 22, 44, 61 (inset), 63, 66, 69, 71R, 72, 112; Royal Collection, Thailand: 105; Sotheby's: 39, 81, 82, 87; Stichting Huis Doorn: 109; Victoria & Albert Museum: 64, 93; Virginia Museum of Fine Arts, Richmond, Bequest of Lillian Thomas Pratt, 1947: 46; The Walters Art Gallery, Baltimore: 43, 46; Wartski, London 55, 56, 68; The Winter Palace, London: 114